RAMBLINGS IN THE FIELD
OF CONSERVATION

By

Dr. ELLIOTT S. BARKER

Author, Conservationist
and Wildlife Consultant

Conservation Pledge

I GIVE MY PLEDGE
AS AN AMERICAN
TO SAVE AND FAITHFULLY
TO DEFEND FROM WASTE
THE NATURAL RESOURCES
OF MY COUNTRY—
ITS AIR, SOIL,
AND MINERALS, ITS
FORESTS, WATERS,
AND WILDLIFE

the sunstone press

FOREWORD

More technological advances and sociological changes occurred in the past 100 years than during any similar period in history, and the author of this book has experience with many of them. Certainly, his personal knowledge of the conservation movement is unique among living Americans.

Elliott Barker moved to New Mexico at the age of three years, travelling with his family in a covered wagon. Now, soon to reach 90, he still is active as an elder statesman of the conservation movement. This book, itself, is a tribute to the author's continuing dedication and stamina. It might be noted that J. Stokley Ligon, in a foreword to another book written by Mr. Barker thirty years ago, said it was "a fitting climax to his years of rugged experience afoot and in the saddle, as rancher and hunter." So, even in 1946, he had achieved eminence in the field of conservation.

My association with Elliott goes back many years, to the time when we served as administrators of wildlife agencies in adjoining states and were active together in efforts of the Western Association of State Game and Fish Commissioners and the International Association of Game, Fish and Conservation Commissioners. I knew him to be vigorous, aggressive, and articulate on matters relating to the conservation of natural resources.

He long has stood and fought for clean air and water, sound wildlife management, and preservation of wilderness values. Recognizing the opportunities presented by concerted efforts, Elliott played a leading role in initiating the National Wildlife Federation—now the world's largest conservation organization.

Few people would be as well qualified as Elliott Barker to write a book on conservation—certainly nobody could cover such a long period of time. As you read it, you will see that he appreciates the intricate inter-relationships of all living things, including the wildlife. Thus, gentleman and scholar, Elliott also is an ecologist and environmentalist. Moreover, he has the capability of making an outdoor experience "come alive" through his picturesque and descriptive writings.

I have shared many of the "Ramblings" outlined in this book, and predict it will be valued as historical reference material for scholars as well as a source of pleasure for those who merely are interested in reading for pleasure.

Thomas L. Kimball
Executive Vice President
National Wildlife Federation

INTRODUCTION

New Mexico's Mr. Conservation in his autobiography gives a graphic insight into why this name has been given to him. Starting with his early boyhood days and ending with his thoughts on the future, it covers throughout the influence he had on the wildlife scene. This impact while more strongly felt in New Mexico, also spreads into national and international circles.

Elliott Barker was friend and co-worker of many of the greats in conservation. He could call Aldo Leopold, Ding Darling, Seth Gordon and Ira Gabrielson as friends. He took an active part in the early days of conservation and the movement is where it is today, because of him and other strong-willed and dedicated men like him.

He gives you an insight as to his thinking, early background years and then takes you through his 22 years as Director of the New Mexico Department of Game and Fish. Throughout the book are related incidents and anecdotes that shows his strong character and dedicated interest in conservation in general and wildlife in particular. Early problems concerning a lack of money, the depression, drought and its affect on wildlife, the battle of Black Canyon Refuge where the first hunting of anterless deer was permitted are all discussed. He lists the various programs that were initiated by him during his tenure, such as providing wildlife for the public land, habitat restoration, the introduction of extinct species and of new exotic species, the biopolitical problems in fisheries management and probably the most widely known item, that of his involvement in the dedication of Smokey Bear as a national symbol for fire protection and wildlife preservation.

He was also vitally involved in national and international programs, in addition to his New Mexico duties. He served three terms as President of the Western Association of State Game and Fish Commissioners, two consecutive terms, something that has never since been duplicated, and during one of these terms he served as President of the International Association of Game, Fish and Conservation Commissioners as well. He helped found the National Wildlife Federation, which now represents a million and a half conservationists throughout this nation. The story relates his long and hard battles for wilderness protection, state's rights and the New Mexico Wildlife Federation.

The book is a tribute to a man whose every breath from his early childhood has been directed toward and influenced by the conservation of our natural resources. I think a passage from the last chapter well tells it all.

"At eighty-nine I might well say that my

future lies behind me to be relived in reminiscences. However, it seems possible my lifelong experiences, and lessons learned in the field of conservation may enable me to still make some contributions for the future. As long as the good Lord permits me to stay around, I am sure that I will not be content to sit back and reminisce. Unfortunately, radically changing times, attitudes and methods in these atomic, jet and Watergate days make it difficult for one of my generation to fit in. . . . There are many formidable problems to be solved. . . . We must have pure air to breathe and pure water to drink. The soil must be conserved . . . and forests must be managed on a sustained yield basis. Adequate wildlife habitat must someway be saved and wilderness areas preserved intact. We must have energy for industries, lights, household facilities and for travel. . . . I have faith that such scientists as those who produced the atomic bomb and energy, filled the air with jets, sent men to walk on the moon . . . can solve the energy problem."

Jesse Williams
Chief of Public Affairs
New Mexico Department of Game & Fish

TABLE OF CONTENTS

CHAPTER 1

How Come You Are A Conservationist?

In 1964 I was presented with the National Wildlife Federation's State Conservationist Of The Year award and the American Motors Corporation's citation, plaque and a five hundred dollar check in recognition of outstanding work in conservation. I was surprised and made to wonder how I could deserve such tributes. Conceding that I had worked hard yet my accomplishments seemed so relatively small.

After the presentation ceremony, a young man said to me, "Mr. Barker, they said you were ranch-raised and had only a high school education. How come you are a conservationist?"

My off-the-cuff answer was, "Perhaps being ranch-raised was a potent factor, and lack of a college education had nothing to do with it."

The young man's question has made me try to identify the contributing factors that caused me to become a dyed-in-the-wool conservationist. To do so I have to start with my childhood days. I was eighth in a family of eleven children—no population conservation about that—only eight of whom lived at home at any one time. We were raised on a small mountain ranch where making a living was hard, hard work. It was an inherent way of life to be conservative of food and clothing.

Going barefooted in summers, as we kids did, was certainly conserving shoes if not sore toes and bruised heels. I recall an expression my mother and father often used at mealtime when we helped ourselves to food as it was passed around the long table. "Be careful that your eyes aren't bigger than your appetite."

There was always plenty of wholesome food to eat, but none to waste. If I left food on my plate it was put in the cupboard—we had no refrigerator—and I would have to eat it at the next meal before taking anything more on my plate. That was an effective lesson in food conservation. Fish and game were an important supplement to the family food supply, and I remember well my first lesson in fish conservation.

2

When I was nine years old, I spent a week with a married sister, Ida Blake, while her husband was away. There was a beautiful, tumbling little trout stream, teeming with cutthroat trout, flowing through the homestead in an isolated canyon. Seldom, if ever, had anyone fished there. My sister sent me with a willow pole, short line and snell hook, to be baited with grasshoppers, to catch a mess of fish.

Every pool had two or three nice trout in it feeding high in the water, just waiting for me to dunk a grasshopper for them to grab. If a kid ever had fun it was me! The trouble was that I didn't know when I had enough trout. My conception of the word "mess" must have been different from what my sister meant. Anyway I took back to the house two long willow stringers of trout—far more than we could eat before they spoiled.

My sister was aghast, but she did not scold. Instead, she said firmly, "Elliott, you shouldn't have taken so many. If everybody did that there would soon be no trout in the stream. The good Lord put them there for us to use but not to waste. If we don't show our appreciation of the Lord's bountiful gifts He might withhold them hereafter." She finished by saying, "Now run down to the creek and clean every one of them, and remember never to take more fish or game than you can use."

My mother preached the same doctrine to

us. She forbade us from taking any game that we did not need, or at a time that it was not in good flesh. That meant no venison from about February until September.

When I was given my first 22 rifle at about age ten it was my father who said, "You must learn to shoot straight so as not to waste ammunition." He did not say be conservation minded with ammunition, but it meant the same thing. Two or three years later when I began to use his 45-70 Winchester, and at first was not a very good marksman with it, he reprimanded me for wasting valuable ammunition.

There were both mule deer and whitetails in the area, but neither was plentiful. We had to hunt hard and carefully to get our wild meat. Mountain lions, on the other hand, were plentiful, and we realized that every mature lion was taking from forty to fifty deer a year. We felt that conservation of the deer supply would be well served by reducing the lion population and that we did. Deer could not be increased by improving their habitat for the optimum primeval conditions had not been impaired.

The Pecos River Forest Reserve, now Santa Fe National Forest, within which our ranch was situated, was established by proclamation of President Harrison in 1892, but was not put under administration until 1898. It was then, when I was twelve years old, that we began hearing about forest conservation, and reading cloth posters on the subject tacked up in strategic places in the area. Emphasis was placed on forest fire prevention. That was easy to understand because there were within six to eight miles of the ranch some vast, burned over areas in the alpine zone.

Very soon after that the regulation of livestock grazing in the forest began in order to protect the areas against overuse which would deplete the forest resources and induce erosion. The need for that kind of conservation was obvious, although many of the large livestock operators resented any regulation of range use.

My father had a small water-powered sawmill, and when I was in my early teens, he purchased some saw timber on the Forest Reserve. We were not allowed to go in and cut whatever tree we might want. Instead, the Forest Ranger selected the mature trees to be cut and marked them. He left the young, healthy timber and enough older trees to provide seed to reforest the area. Then we were required to lop off all the limbs from the tops of the trees felled and carefully pile all the brush in safe places where it could be burned in wet weather and reduce the danger of a forest fire later. That was a lesson in forest conservation.

All these things, I believe, instilled in me

the basic conception that conservation of natural resources was right and necessary. Then, in 1909, when I became a U.S. Forest Ranger, it was brought home to me through administration policies and the admonitions of the Chief Forester, Gifford Pinchot, in his writings.

In 1912 and 1913, I had the rare privilege of working as Forest Ranger under Aldo Leopold, Supervisor of the Carson National Forest. In the brief period of my service under him he gave me effective inspiration in the field of conservation, especially in conservation and management of wildlife. I have always considered it a great privilege to have worked under, and later associated with, that wonderful man who later became Dr. Aldo Leopold, America's greatest authority on wildlife managment.

These, I believe, are the early steps that I took up the conservation ladder to become a dyed-in-the-wood conservationist. It's been a rewarding experience, during which my boyhood love of God's great outdoors acquired on that little ranch far up in the New Mexico's rocky Sangre de Cristo Mountains has never diminished.

CHAPTER TWO

Ten Years Forest Service Experience

My first assignment as an Assistant U.S. Forest Ranger on January 1, 1909, was at Cuba, New Mexico, on a new addition to the west side of the Jemez (now Santa Fe) National Forest. Much of the area was not typical national forest type. Instead it was piñon and juniper timber and open sagebrush country. Up to that time there had been no restriction or regulation of livestock grazing or timber cutting on these public lands.

The result was that the country was badly overgrazed, and with the depletion of the forage ground cover soil erosion was prevalent.

7

Being in a remote area sixty miles from a railroad, timber cutting had been limited to local needs for house logs, fence material, timber for one little sawmill and dead wood for fuel. Hence, no great damage had been done to timber resources. Forest fire hazard on my district was not great, but we occasionally had a small fire to put out. I got some good forest fire fighting experience on an adjoining district under an old ranger.

In the name of conservation it was our duty to bring the use of all renewable natural resources under such regulation as would prevent further damage and preserve them for sustained benefit of legitimate users. That meant livestock numbers had to be reduced to the carrying capacity of the ranges, and the numbers permitted to be grazed distributed equitably among the settlers rather than being usurped by a few large owners.

The population of the area was ninety-nine percent Spanish-American, many of whom were illiterate and very few spoke any English. That made our job a formidable one. The fact that I spoke Spanish fluently was a tremendous asset. My companion ranger spoke no Spanish and was behind the eight ball much of the time. Conditions in the district were such that my fellow ranger and I were instructed to ride and work together at all times, and never go anywhere without our sidearms. Fortunately, we never had to use them.

Selling the natural resource conservation concept was not easy. However, the general populace was more amenable to the new order than the few in higher educational, financial and political brackets. The few large stock owners, including a powerful political boss, resented the creation of the National Forest and any interference with their use of the public lands and resources. They challenged our authority and dealt us all the misery they could. With the backing of the Forest Supervisor and U.S. District Attorney, we won out.

My contribution to the cause of conservation on that district was that we pioneered among uninformed people and laid a solid foundation for our successors to build on.

After ten months on that district I was transferred to the Pecos National Forest (now Pecos Division Santa Fe N. F.). I was happy to get into a better situation, and the Pecos district, embracing the major portion of what is now the Pecos Wilderness Area, suited me perfectly. It had been under Interior Department Forest Reserve administration from 1898 to 1905, and under Department of Agriculture Forest Service administration from then on. The ground work of forest conservation had been well laid.

The headwaters of the Pecos River, including many small streams, rise in a huge, horseshoe-shaped basin formed by two prongs of the Sangre de Cristo Mountain Range, the elevation ranges from 7,000 to over 13,000 feet, and the annual precipitation varies from 14 inches to over 30 inches in the high country. The annual water production for domestic, municipal and irrigation use is about an acre foot for every acre of land. Hence, in a dry state, protection of the watershed is of very great importance.

Conservation of the watershed was then the most important item in the administration program and remains so today. Maintenance of a good ground cover to prevent erosion and absorb all the rain and snow water possible to come out in clear springs to fee the streams was, and still is, imperative. That was our number one conservation obligation. Forest fires in the alpine timber type destroy the ground mulch and do great damage. Several old burned over areas provided impressive examples. Overgrazing was another hazard to the watershed.

During my three years on that district, due to diligent fire prevention efforts, we had no forest fires of any consequence. Overgrazing in some areas we did have. Settlers in the narrow valleys around the perimeter of the forest had used the area for summer grazing their livestock long before the national forest was created. They were dependent on it to supplement their meager livelihood. Reduction of cattle and sheep numbers without hurting the permittees' economic status was exceedingly difficult. That was a serious conservation problem to solve.

The most serious damage was by sheep grazing on the high elevation slopes causing soil erosion. We took up slack everyway we could—got some permittees to reduce numbers, others to replace sheep with cattle—and we supervised the range use carefully to keep sheep off of vulnerable areas, and closed some damaged areas to sheep grazing. Based on the start we made, all sheep grazing on the upper Pecos River watershed has now been eliminated. A few scars, not large enough to be of importance, remain.

The area has always been an important wildlife habitat. The indigenous elk and bighorn sheep had been exterminated, but mule deer, black bear, turkeys, grouse, mountain lions, bobcats and coyotes remained. Grizzly bears were so destructive to livestock that very few were left. The organic act, creating the Forest Service, required it to cooperate in game law enforcement and all rangers carried commissions as deputy game wardens. Thus a part of our work was wildlife conservation.

We discussed restoration of elk and bighorn sheep with the State Game Warden, but nothing was accomplished at that time. Possibly we planted the seed that resulted in both being restored later—elk in 1915 and bighorns in 1967. We did assume the job of distributing the trout fry provided by the U.S. Bureau of

Fisheries. Some had to be taken in five-gallon cans on pack animals to stock inaccessible streams.

Also the forest service was sometimes called upon to assist in elimination of predators, such as bears and cougars, doing damage to livestock. I once took four male cougars that had killed three mares and fifteen colts belonging to a permittee on my district. Any assignment pertaining to wildlife always delighted me.

My work also included marking of timber and scaling of saw logs on timber sales. We had some railroad tie and piling timber sales and the selection of that size trees to be cut was very difficult. We tolerated no clear cutting, but tried to leave enough tie and piling size trees to grow into a good stand of saw timber. That didn't please the purchasers. They wanted it all. We stood firm and practiced forest conservation and management in accordance with good silvicultural practices. Tom Stewart was my supervisor and always backed me.

While on that district I met the prettiest teen-age girl I had ever seen, daughter of H. S. Arnold, a local rancher. On May 17, 1911, when she was near eighteen, I married her. She has proved to be a loyal wife and has been putting up with me for sixty-five years. Amazing!

After three years on the Pecos district I

was transferred, against my will, to the Carson National Forest. It turned out to be the best thing that could have happened to me. It gave me the privilege of working, though briefly, under Supervisor Aldo Leopold and circumstances provided the opportunity for rapid advancement. My contacts with Dr. Leopold there and my association with him in after years were a great inspiration in conservation, especially wildflife conservation and management.

The Carson Forest is in three divisions, the Taos, Amarilla and Jicarilla. The latter two are in the southern extremities of the San Juan Mountains adjacent to the Colorado line, and Taos is only a short distance from the Colorado line, in the rugged Sangre de Cristo mountains. My first assignment was on the Amarilla Division, largest of the three.

There was much open grass country on this division and livestock grazing was our major concern, for there were large numbers of both cattle and sheep permitted to graze in summer. The country was generally overgrazed, particularly in the lower ranges used for lambing grounds. To add to the overgrazing and erosion problem, the whole country was heavily infested with prairie dogs, not just in towns but it was like a boundless prairie dog Megalopolis.

The prairie dog diggings and forage consumption not only damaged the lands but also reduced the range carrying capacity for live-stock. Wholesale eradication had not been initiated there at that time but came on some years later and was a blessing.

Forest fire prevention and suppression, of course, took precedence over everything else, but actually did not consume very much of a ranger's time. There were some small timber sales where timber had to be marked, sometimes on snowshoes in winter, and logs scaled regularly, but grazing work took up most of my time working out ways to conserve forage grazing resources and stop erosion.

Up to that time several bands of sheep from 500 to 1,000 head belonging to different owners were assigned to graze on community allotments. This resulted in close herding and trailing herds too much. It also encouraged the bedding of sheep more than one night in the same spot, which was prohibited because it would damage the area. When a ranger would take herders to task for violation of the bedding and other rules they would always blame other herders using the same allotment.

To overcome these difficulties and as a means of improving range use, I worked out, with the supervisor's approval, a system of individual allotments, mapped them and described the boundaries by topographic features so that they could be readily understood, some I wrote in Spanish. This made each permittee responsible for making the best use possible of his allotment and preventing unnecessary damage.

At first there was vigorous protests, each permittee claiming that he had been discriminated against in the size or quality of the allotment assigned to him. Naturally some mistakes were made and a few boundary changes had to be made. However, it was not long until both herders and permittees came to like the new system. It worked so well on my district that I was given a two-months assignment on an adjoining district to assist the ranger in working out an individual allotment system there.

Of course, this was not a cure-all for there were just too many sheep on the forest. It did give us far better control and enabled us to place the blame for unnecessary damage and violations of the rules and regulations where it belonged. I believe devising that system was my biggest contribution to range conservation.

An influential permittee who had two allotments put pressure on us to issue permits to two sheep-owner friends of his who had no prior grazing privileges in the Forest. When told that there simply was not any surplus range he said, "Oh yes there is plenty. You just don't know the country like I do."

I said, "All right, we will assign one band to graze on each of your allotments." I knew that he would be glad to have them anywhere else but not on his allotments.

He looked at me with a sheepish grin and said, "Here son, have a cigar. You've got more sense than I thought you had."

After two years on that district, I was transferred to the Supervisor's office in Taos, and was given a special assignment. The job was classification of the lands of the Amarilla and Jicarilla divisions of the Forest, and it took the better part of a year to complete it. The object was to compile detailed information on the use to which the lands were best adapted— timber production, grazing, agriculture, etc. It did not involve map making, but instead, spotting on existing maps in color the various types of land, supplemented by descriptive text.

Under the Act of June 11, 1906, homesteading within National Forests was permitted where it could be shown that the lands were suitable for agriculture, and better adapted to that than to any other use. We were pestered by many homestead applications where there was no possibility of agricultural success. Tracts as small as twenty acres could be homesteaded if they qualified otherwise. Many marginal tracts were patented and then abandoned leaving undesirable units of privately owned land scattered through the forest lands. Wisely, the law was later repealed.

Land conservation, I believe, included devotion of lands to the use to which they are best adapted. Certainly my year's work on that land classification project, and handling of many homestead applications gave me a basic environmental perspective which proved of great value to me in forestry, ranch and wildlife conservation work.

When the land classification job was completed in 1915, I was promoted to Deputy Forest Supervisor under Supervisor, Raymond E. Marsh, who climbed the forestry ladder to the top rungs. Because I spoke Spanish fluently, I was able to be of much assistance to Supervisor Marsh, in dealing with the Spanish-American forest users, particularly the grazing permittees. We were engaged in a program of reduction of sheep to the carrying capacity of the ranges to prevent further overgrazing damage and cure that which had already been done.

A vexing problem was that large operators had many bands of sheep, from a few hundred to a thousand, on *partido* contracts. That is, share contracts whereby local land owners who could qualify for grazing permits but who had no livestock would be given a band of sheep to take care of as if they owned them, and then give the owner a share of the lambs at weaning time each year. The share men would apply for the permits in their own names and claim that they owned the sheep. Thus, the big owners would actually enjoy grazing privileges for numbers of sheep far in

17

excess of the maximum limit.

We had to put a stop to that subterfuge, but actual ownership was hard to establish. If we did prove our case the permit had to be cancelled. That didn't hurt the owner as much as it did the share man, who then would have to seek other means of making a living. Usually, the owner had a sizable permit in his own name and that could be reduced and the share man continue his operation with the permit in the actual owner's name.

We were in the midst of these programs when Supervisor Marsh's father died. Supervisor Marsh took a year's leave of absence to clean up his father's business. The position of Acting Supervisor, with the responsibility of carrying on all operations, was suddenly and unexpectedly thrust upon me. I proceeded with the Supervisor's programs and policies the best I could in his absence, made some progress and experienced no difficulties.

Mr. Marsh returned at the end of his year's leave, and remained only a couple of months when he was transferred to the Coconino National Forest in Arizona. I was then appointed Supervisor upon the recommendation of Paul G. Reddington, Regional Forester. He assured me that he would back me up in the program of reducing livestock to the carrying capacity of the ranges. Some big livestock permittees tried to take advantage of me, a young man of thirty, but they failed.

18

We had made a lot of progress in the conservation of the range when the First World War broke out in April 1917. Then we got a jolt that rattled our molars! The Secretary of Agriculture issued instructions to waive the grazing regulations and to issue permits to almost anyone who wanted to put stock on the forest. The reason he gave was to produce more meat for the war effort. It was a ridiculous policy, causing us to lose in one swoop all the ground we had gained, and harmed the war effort rather than helping it. Our protests were futile.

More sheep and cattle went on the range and fewer went to market. Livestock prices soared, but in hopes they would go still higher many lambs, calves and aging animals that would ordinarily have gone to market were held over to be summer grazed on the forest. While the war ended in November 1918, those temporary permits were extended over the 1919 season. Then the bottom dropped out of the market and sheep and cattlemen were caught in a terrible bind. Most of them went broke.

We lost more than we had gained in range restoration, fewer cattle and sheep went to market, and the range was badly damaged. One of the biggest sheepmen who had plunged deeply could not meet his obligations and stood to lose everything he had. So he went out in his garage and blew his brains out with a 45 Colt revolver.

All our efforts at range improvement had gone with the wind, and the wind really blows in that country!

As had been stated, forest fire prevention and suppression took precedence over all other activities. The fall of 1917 was unusually dry, and the winds were persistent. All fire lookout stations were fully manned up until late November. Some of my regular staff were in the armed forces, and most of the experienced lookout men were either in the armed forces or war work. I was not sure how dependable some of the inexperienced lookout men were.

One morning we could see smoke boiling up only a few miles from one of the lookouts on the Amarilla Division. The lookout man had not reported the fire, so I called him by phone and asked him if he had gone to the tower and checked that morning. He assured me that he had and that all was clear. I said, "Hurry and check again."

Soon he called back and exclaimed, "Gee sus cripes, the whole world is afire." We had a new lookout man there the next day.

Late in November I made an inspection of the Gold Hill timberline lookout station in the rugged Taos Mountains, and spent the night with the lookout man. He seemed to be doing his job faithfully. I went with him to the tower next morning at sunrise. We could see no smoke. The wind was strong from the west and any smoke beyond a shoulder of the mountain would be flattened out and harder to see than if it were boiling up.

Leaving Gold Hill early I rode south along the rugged, timberline divide for a long way to drop off into the Taos Pueblo Canyon and on down it to Taos. In mid-afternoon I came to the end of the high country and looked off into the head of a canyon below. I was astounded to see a hot, two-acre fire partly in an old burn and partly in the alpine forest. I hastened to it and checked it out. Being whipped by a strong wind I could see that there was nothing I could do but go for help. But first I checked to see how the fire started as there was no lightning. On the windward side next to the green timber I found where an Indian had camped, dressed a deer taken out of season and left his campfire burning.

I then hastened toward Taos, but it got dark and I missed the intended route. I had to work my way, leading my horse, down a very steep, cliffy hillside. I finally made it and at about ten PM. I reached the Taos Indian Pueblo three miles from Taos. I roused an Indian friend and had him alert the Pueblo Governor and Council for a meeting with me at midnight to make plans to put out the fire.

I hurried on into Taos and called all my available staff, and put them to recruiting a crew of twenty-five men, assembling fire tools—axes, crosscut saws, shovels, rakes and grubbing hoes—groceries and camp equipment. I knew that with the wind blowing as it was we'd need a big crew to control the fire. Of course we'd have to have saddle and pack horses to carry men and equipment to the fire scene. They had a formidable job to do between midnight and dawn.

Ranger Carrol Dwire went back with me to the Pueblo where the Governor and War Chief had assembled the Council. The deliberateness of the proceedings irritated me, but the Indians could not be hurried.

The Governor, through an interpreter, questioned me about the route I had come down. I explained about the rugged route I had followed and he said, "No, you can't come down that way."

I said, "Yes, but I did only four hours ago."

He said, "Well, at night in dark maybe come down. In daylight no."

Anyway, after they made me promise to feed the crew well and provide bedding (which we always did) they agreed to send a crew of twenty-five men, and to be ready to start at daylight. My men did a fabulous job of getting ready.

By daylight we were ready to start for the fire with twenty-five men and a dozen pack horses. I had only taken time out long enough to go home, get something to eat and tell my wife what was up. The Indians were not yet ready when we passed the Pueblo, but soon

22

followed with the Governor and War Chief leading.

That forest fire was the worst and hardest to bring under control of any that I have ever battled. It crowned out in the spruce and fir timber and finally covered over six hundred acres. By daylight the third day we had it whipped. It had taken long hours with strenuous work and smoke-filled lungs to do it. If I had not insisted upon haste and a big crew of men, that fire might have destroyed ten times that much forest.

I went to camp, ate a big bowl of oatmeal and rolled up in a *sugan* just as the sun was coming up. When I awoke the sun was just setting. I got up and ate supper and went right to bed again and slept all night. I had gone seventy-two hours without closing my eyes.

In October and November 1918 the terrible flu epidemic which oldtimers will remember hit Taos worse than any other place in the United States. I happened to be president of the Taos County Red Cross, and the burden of relief efforts fell on me. It was an attempt at a human conservation job. We obtained the services of six doctors and nine nurses from St. Louis, and turned a church and a school house into hospitals. Our efforts to save lives were mostly in vain. No one knew what to do with that particular type of flu.

Strong, healthy people were well one day, sick the next and dead the next or the day after. In sixty days we buried ten percent of the Taos County population—twelve hundred and fifty souls. But that is too morbid a story for this book.

In the spring of 1909 I got homesick for ranch life. I'd bought my father's old homestead and some nearby property which would qualify me for a permit to summer-graze a hundred head of cattle on the National Forest. So I resigned my position of Forest Supervisor and moved back to my old stomping ground.

All the misfortunes, fortunes, disappointments and opportunities which awaited my family and me could not possibly have been predicted, and much less the horrors that have been conferred upon me.

CHAPTER THREE

Conservation on a Mountain Ranch

I was enthusiastic on April 1, 1919, when we moved back to my old home on Sapello Creek in the Sangre de Cristo Mountains to try my hand at ranching, but my good wife, Ethel, was more than a bit skeptical of the advisability of the change we were making. We realized that schooling for our children, Roy, seven, and Florence, five, would be a problem. Perhaps my deep-rooted ties to the area and my exuberance of being back home again blinded me to some important realities.

However, this is not the story of the ups and downs on a mountain ranch, but rather

25

it's about what the mountain rancher was able to do by way of wildlife and other natural resource conservation. I soon found that making a decent living for my family kept me too busy to do many other things that I had planned on doing. Yet there were some overlapping aspects of ranching and conservation and some things worthy of note, I believe, were accomplished.

For instance, my wife's project was to raise a hundred turkeys for the Thanksgiving and Christmas market. For her to do so required me to do intensive coyote and other predator control which greatly helped wild turkeys and deer to survive in adjacent areas. Conservative use of the mountain range with my cattle insured forage for deer and elk to thrive on. Resisting the temptation to divert all the creek water needed for irrigation in dry periods, saved the trout. Permitting five hundred acres of my land to be used, along with national forest lands, for game refuge purposes helped to build up the deer and turkey populations.

That general mountain area was always good habitat for mule and whitetail deer, elk, black bear, turkeys and blue grouse. Predators, such as cougars, coyotes and bobcats were also indigenous to the area, and sometimes became too plentiful. While riding the range looking after my cattle I very soon discovered that the whitetail deer had, for some mysterious reason, become almost extinct. Mule deer were at a very low ebb and wild turkeys were almost gone. Elk, once exterminated from the state, had been restored to the Pecos watershed and were beginning to establish themselves on the Lone Tree, Beaver Creek and Big Burn areas where I summer-grazed my cattle. Cougar, coyote and black bear signs were about normal.

After a year there I decided that something must be done to build up the dwindling game supply. I found out that there had been considerable poaching. The Game Department's financial status enabled it to employ only two or three game wardens to patrol and enforce the game laws over the entire state. I had retained my deputy game warden commission when I resigned my position in the Forest Service and it was renewed each year. I put the word out that illegal killing of game in that area must be stopped, and warned that I would have to prosecute any poacher that I might catch.

That stopped most of the illegal killing of game, and a prosecution helped. A good friend and neighbor had to be prosecuted twice, once for turkey and once for deer killing, before he got the message. In the second case the judge withheld his 30-06 rifle for six months. That was a daily reminder that he'd better mend his ways. I had warned him and treated him fairly and he never ceased to be my friend.

I decided that a good game refuge would hasten the restoration of game. So I mapped out an area of about 25 sections (square miles) with Sapello Creek, three miles of which flowed through my property, as the north boundary. Thus, I could control access from both the north and west. With my neighbors and forest service joining me, establishment of the refuge was recommended, and the State Game Commission established it. The carrying of firearms on the refuge was prohibited. The refuge was well respected and supplemented by coyote and cougar control quickly became effective in building up the mule deer and Merriam turkey populations. While little of the refuge was included in my cattle range, I established and maintained salt grounds anyway. The increase in mule deer was noticeable within two or three years.

I raised oats mixed with field peas for winter hay for my cattle. The after crop left in the fields provided a lot of grain and pea leaves for fall and early spring wild turkey feed. While most of the turkeys wintered a few miles south, some remained and fed at my cattle feeding grounds on shattered grain. My fields and hay stacks were all on the refuge, but the turkeys often crossed the creek to feed and roost on the south exposures of the canyon. There, in season, they were fair game for licensed hunters, and it became a very popular hunting ground. The increase in wild turkeys was phenomenal!

While the new food supply helped a great deal to increase the turkey population, I am sure that the control of predators, principally coyotes, had more to do with it. We found that to get to market with a hundred turkeys we had to start with two hundred poults old enough to follow the flocks into the fields to forage. Despite my diligent control of coyotes with rifle and traps they would get away with nearly a hundred. Great horned owls and bobcats took a few.

It seems obvious when coyotes are that hard on domestic turkeys, despite dogs, rifle and traps, they must be mighty hard on wild turkeys with none of those hazards to contend with. We found that one could not do selective control, that is, just kill certain coyotes that were killers, which we hear so much about from sentimentalists. I would get rid of every coyote in the vicinity and in a couple of weeks there would be that many more come in, and they all liked turkeys.

Anyway, with the aid of a refuge, a new food supply and predator control we built up the wild turkeys from a few stragglers to great abundance in a six year period. It remained so until several years after I left the ranch.

Some people suspect that some of our domestic turkeys wandered off and took up with the wild ones and that was the reason for the rapid increase. I am sure that is not the case. We did lose a few that way, but it has been well established that domestic turkeys are less hardy and so much less astute that they are incapable of surviving in the wild state against predator hazards and the difficulty of having to make their own living. Today the methods employed in my notable success in wild turkey restoration and conservation might well be followed by game departments in the many areas where these fine birds have reached a deplorably low ebb.

Deer responded to cougar and coyote control, law enforcement and refuge protection, and within seven or eight years had not only stocked the refuge but adjacent areas as well. As of this writing, due to abolition of the refuge, poaching and lack of cougar and coyote control both deer and turkeys are again at a pitifully low population level.

While I was in the U.S. Forest Service I found that ranchers living within the forest can render valuable services in forest fire suppression in their areas. By keeping an eye out for smoke they can often detect a fire while it is small before the lookout man or ranger can, and get to it quicker. Getting to a fire quickly with men enough to put it out will save many acres from burning and reduce costs and effort.

Therefore, when I went to the ranch I volunteered to act as a cooperative fire warden in my area. During the eleven years I was on

30

the ranch my family, employees and I discovered at least a half dozen forest fires. I got to them with men and equipment long before the ranger did and usually had them under control without his help. It was a great satisfaction for the ranger to know that he could depend on me, and I was more than glad to help him out that way.

Having worked so hard while I was in the forest service to stop overgrazing, and for proper handling of livestock on the ranges, I was rather on the spot when I, myself, became a grazing permittee. In other words, it was now up to me to practice what I'd preached. My grazing permit was for a hundred head of cattle from May 1 to October 15. I had the advantage of having an individual allotment, but it was unfenced and I was pestered occasionally by considerable numbers of cattle coming in from other areas. It contributed to excessive grazing and required a lot of extra riding to keep them off.

My allotment included Beaver Creek and a big, burned-over area in higher country. To utilize these types of range properly required rotation grazing, that is, use the lower range in spring and fall and high country range in midsummer. To keep my cattle on the high range I had to build a pole fence across a narrow canyon separating the two ranges. The Beaver Creek range was used for two months in the spring and a month and a half in the fall, and the high country during the July and August rainy season.

The spring range would be grazed pretty close but by fall it was lush with rank grass everywhere, and the cattle put on extra fat on it. There was still some time for the high country grass to recover from its two months use. With that system it was possible to keep all ranges in excellent condition and to have extra fat cows and very heavy calves.

We all loved that country for it was wonderful for outdoor enjoyment. My wife and our children often accompanied me on horseback while looking after the cattle. Roy and Florence grew up that way. Our youngest daughter, who came along in 1921, at six began to follow me all day on Spike, an absolutely trustworthy saddle horse.

At about eleven, Roy and a boy friend the same age, found a little spotted fawn on Beaver Creek and carried it home on their horses to keep for a pet. That was not a good wildlife management practice and actually was against the law. We fed and cared for the fawn overnight, then next morning I made them take it back and leave it exactly where they had found it. I was sure the mother would stick around close by and find it. That taught them a lesson in wildlife ethics.

Bill Koogler, a neighbor, and I were in the Big Burn area looking after cattle and came across a doe fighting off a coyote that was trying to catch and kill her fawn. I took a shot at the coyote with my 45 Colt revolver but I missed, and he ran into the timber for cover. We rode on and the doe and fawn stayed right there close to the trail as if they knew they were safe from the coyote in our presence. When we came back by that afternoon the doe was gone, but the half-eaten remains of the fawn were there. Why sympathize with a trapped coyote?

Two or three coyotes, sometimes one alone, summer and winter, would chase a full-grown doe or buck until their prey was completely exhausted and would stop in a creek or other canyon bottom. There they would worry it down, perhaps hamstring it, and then go for the neck and make the kill. Many, many times have I seen where that happened. Coyotes and cougars alike will kill strong, healthy deer, not just the weak and sick ones, as is often claimed. That is not conjecture, but it is personal observation over a long period of years.

In 1914 the New Mexico Game Protective Association was organized in Silver City for the purpose of helping the Game Department and Forest Service to protect and restore wildlife and to secure passage of needed better game laws. It is still functioning today, but the name has been changed to New Mexico Wildlife Federation. It always has been made up of local chapters throughout the state. I

33

had been a charter member of the Taos GPA, and was disappointed to find that there was no GPA in Las Vegas, our trading point. With the help of some sportmen friends a chapter was organized there. The organization has had its ups and downs, but is still listed as an affiliate of the New Mexico Wildlife Federation. It gave me valuable support in my law enforcement work.

In the mid 1920's I had the honor and great pleasure of having Aldo Leopold visit me overnight at the ranch. We talked until late about wildlife and the future of the Department of Game and Fish which was then pretty much involved in politics. He was very active in the New Mexico Game Protective Association at that time.

In 1926 Mr. Leopold had me go to Santa Fe and meet with him and the State Game Commission. They begged me to accept the position of Executive Secretary to the Game Warden, with the promise of appointing me State Game Warden at the termination of the current Game Warden's term. My situation at the ranch was such that I could see no way to accept. It was with great regrets that I had to decline the offer. In bidding me goodbye, Mr. Leopold said, "Someday you will fill that position."

We had good times and bad on the ranch. It was hard going from the 1920 recession until 1925 when cattle prices went up steadily.

We did well from 1925 until the crash of 1929 preceding the great depression. Most cattle and sheep men went broke. So did most of the banks. In the early spring of 1930 we were flat broke and decided that we had had enough of ranching. We sold all our cattle, almost gave them away, leased the ranch for a pittance, and I set out looking for a job.

Work of any kind was unbelievably hard to get. The Game Department rejected my application for a field warden job. The Forest Service said they would be glad to have me, but conditions were very bad and I would have to start at the bottom again. I didn't relish that! In 1926 Mr. Harry Chandler, publisher of the Los Angeles Times, had offered me a good position as wildlife manager of his Vermejo Park property in northern New Mexico. Conditions on the ranch were so good that I had to decline the offer.

Vermejo Park was a three hundred sixty thousand-acre cattle ranch and game preserve in a wondrous mountain country. While continuing to operate it as a cattle ranch, Mr. Chandler had sold 96 memberships in the Vermejo Club, which he had organized, to prominent people at five thousand dollars each. They would have hunting, fishing and other recreational privileges. Now I applied to Mr. Chandler for a job.

Mr. Chandler wrote back, "We need you, but the financial situation is such that we can't offer you a salary that you would accept."

I wrote back and said, "Just make me an offer and see."

His offer was a hundred and fifty dollars a month, a house to live in, a milch cow, some chickens and saddle horses and their feed. I gladly accepted the offer and reported for work on April 1, 1930.

CHAPTER FOUR

A Year at Vermejo Park

During the school term of 1929-1930, my wife was living in Las Vegas to keep the children in school. I went to Vermejo Park alone, taking only a camp outfit and my three hunting dogs. I was assigned to a three-room cabin at Castle Rock cow camp where I batched until school was out. Then I drove my Durant car to Las Vegas and brought Ethel and our two daughters to the crude, plumbingless cabin. Ethel never complained except she was lonesome for Roy, who had taken a summer job. I had the bare necessities for housekeeping trucked up from the ranch.

I'd been advised my job would be concerned with wildlife and predator control, law enforcement and guiding fishermen and hunters. Specifically, Mr. Chandler wrote me, "Our deer are steadily decreasing. Hunting can't be responsible since we have had very little of it. I want you to find out what the cause is and correct it if possible."

Neither the ranch superintendent nor the cattle foreman could give me any clue as to the cause of the decline in the deer population, but agreed that it was seriously decreasing. So during my first week there I rode far and wide over the deer and cougar (mountain lions we call them) habitat. Never in my life had I seen so much lion sign. Male lion scrapes were abundant, and my dogs, Pup, Puse and Queenie, located for me the remains of many old carcasses of deer killed by lions. Since lions cover their kills with forest debris, even old kills may be positively identified.

My conclusion was that there had been an unusual concentration of lions on the ranch for several years and that they were decimating the deer population. To correct the situation, as Mr. Chandler had requested, it was up to me to drastically reduce the lion population. That I set out to do, but there was so much other work to be done—patroling boundaries of the property to prevent poaching, taking care of guests, repairing ditches to some fishing lakes—that I only took one female lion and two tom lions that summer. Winter hunting would be easier anyway.

Wildlife conservation and management requires keeping the animals, of whatever species they may be, in balance with their food supply. When deer or elk exceed their food supply they must be reduced in numbers, usually by hunting, to the carrying capacity of the range. Just so with predators, when they begin to deplete their food supply, they too must be reduced, but not exterminated. Lions here were taking far more deer than the annual increase and reducing their numbers was sound wildlife conservation.

I found that coyotes were taking only a few deer, but they and bobcats were hard on the wild turkeys, so they were included in my predator control activities. During the year I was there I took a total of sixteen lions, forty-six coyotes and thirty-nine bobcats. Three lions were taken on the ranch by another hunter and several others on adjacent property.

The propriety and effectiveness of this operation is verified by the fact that the deer population in a few years reached the carrying capacity of the range, and with prudent lion control, remained so up until very recent years when again there has been a drastic decline. I suspect that excessive numbers of predators is the cause.

The original owner and developer of Vermejo Park, Mr. W. H. Bartlett, in 1911, re-established elk which had been exterminated from the state in the 1890's. Now there was a sizable, thriving herd. Beaver were very abundant, and ponds, large and small, made by their dams greatly enhanced the fishing resources and attractiveness of the area. Those industrious dam builders are real conservationists.

I had some game law violations to contend with, including prosecutions, but experienced no difficulties. However, the cattle foreman, Skeet Williams, who also held a deputy game warden commission, caught three men dressing an illegally killed elk and attempted to arrest them. Some way they got the drop on him with their rifles, took his revolver, unsaddled his horse and turned it loose, knowing that he would be unable to catch it, and sent him on his way, ten miles to camp, in his high-heeled boots. Imagine a cowboy walking ten miles!

On the fourth of July we had a bad forest fire. The boss had me take charge and put it out. It was an afternoon and all night job with half a dozen men helping me. Forest conservation was a part of the Park's policy.

My work was most interesting, and involved many adventures, some wild ones, but that has all been related in my book, *When the Dogs Bark "Treed."*

In early March, 1931, a State Senator

friend advised me that there was certain to be a change in the State Game Commission and State Game Warden as soon as the Legislature's term was over, and suggested that I apply for the position of State Game Warden if I was interested. I was very deeply interested, and at once sent my application to the Governor to be given to the Chairman of the Commission if, or when, a new one was appointed.

Colin Neblett, a Federal District Judge, was appointed Chairman and I drove to Santa Fe and conferred with him. The Governor had already given him my application. He suggested that I get some endorsements from the people who knew of my abilities, if any, but none from political sources. That pleased me for I did not want a political job. The Chairman assured me that if I were appointed it would have to be free from politics.

It was a Democratic administration, but my endorsements included some prominent Republicans as well as Democrats who knew of my experience and record. Mr. Talley, under whom I'd worked at Vermejo Park, and many sportsmen sent good letters. But the one I valued most highly was from Dr. Aldo Leopold.

In due time the other two commissioners were appointed, a meeting was held, and I was notified that I'd been appointed State Game Warden (Director, Dept. of Game and Fish), and to report for work on April first. Dr.

Leopold's prediction had come true!

I was the first completely non-political State Game Warden, and by conducting the Department of Game and Fish free of political influences in every respect, I held that position for twenty-two years until I retired in 1953.

CHAPTER FIVE

Conservation Opportunities and Challenges

It was with mixed feelings that I accepted the grave responsibilities inherent to the head of the Department of Game and Fish, a position I had long aspired to, and one in which my friends, including Dr. Leopold, felt that I could be successful. Great opportunities for wildlife conservation accomplishments were there, but the challenges were formidable. Better living conditions for the family, and schools for the children would be a great improvement over our personal situation. Could I adjust to a desk job and forego my cherished outdoor activities? No, not entirely.

Perhaps I could do a better job by dividing my time fifty-fifty between office and field anyway.

A strong Game Commission would back me, but could we free the Department from political influences which had hitherto hampered it? Could we restore lost species of wildlife? Could we build up the low population of deer and antelope to optimum numbers? Could we reduce local overpopulations of deer despite public sentiment against killing of antlerless deer? Could we establish and maintain good cooperative relations, necessary for success, with ranchers, federal agencies and sportsmen's organizations?

How could we build and operate fish hatcheries to adequately stock our streams with our limited finances? How could we possibly maintain an adequate force with our very limited revenue, about a hundred thousand dollars a year?

These and many other questions plagued me. In asking for the job of solving them they had seemed less formidable. Now that I had the position there was nothing to do but buckle down and do my best.

Up until then the Game Commission had been invested with only limited powers. The Legislature had always set the seasons and bag limits and made the rules pertaining thereto. The Legislature, just adjourned, had repealed all such laws and passed an act, long sought by the organized sportsmen, giving the State Game Commission full authority to promulgate all rules and regulations pertaining to wildlife management, including setting of seasons and bag limits, but not setting license fees. The regulations would have the force and effect of law.

Thus, our first job was to formulate a code of rules and regulations for the management of wildlife and fisheries resources. Commissioners James B. McGhee and Gilberto Espinosa put in long hours helping me with that task. We held a public hearing with sportsmen, the Forest Service and interested individuals on our tentative draft. There were some controversial items, particularly on hunting and fishing seasons and correcting the over stocked Black Canyon deer area. With some amendments the code was adopted. The new law has been rated as one of the best in the nation.

If I were to be successful I knew that I had to have the best staff possible. I retained some of the employees of the previous administration, some resigned and I had to replace others. With the salaries we could pay, $150.00 a month for district wardens and trout hatchery foremen, it had to be a labor of love. That is just the kind of staff I wound up with. A more devoted, hard working, clockless crew no one ever had!

The political challenge came at the end of

the first month. It may seem unbelievable, but at that time, regardless of which political party was in power, state employees were assessed two percent of their salaries to support the party. I refused to pay the assessment and would not permit any department employee to pay it. The collector insisted that I would be forced to pay, but I stood pat.

Next day the Democratic state chairman called on me and said, "There is no alternative, you and all department employees will have to pay the assessment if you stay on the payroll."

I said, "We are greatly underpaid, yet we are working twelve to fifteen hours a day to make the Department a success. That will be our contribution to the state and the party. None of us got our jobs through political channels, and we will pay tribute to no party."

Arguing got the chairman nowhere. Finally he said, "I'm sorry, but you and your men will soon be out of your jobs."

The very next day the Governor called me to his office and explained that the two percent assessment policy was standard for both parties, and that he would tolerate no exceptions. I explained my position as I had to the state chairman. He said he would give me a month to think it over, but we'd have to pay or else—.

When the Game Commissioners met I advised them of the score. Commissioner

McGhee said, "Mr. Chairman, I move we go down and work the Governor over."

Without putting the motion to a vote, Judge Neblett, the Chairman, said, "Meeting recessed for an hour."

They had it hot and heavy with the Governor, and at one point all offered their resignations. It so happened that Judge Neblett was powerful politically behind the scenes, and the Governor could not afford to lose his support. Finally, the Governor agreed to make an exception of the Department of Game and Fish. The Commission assured me that I would not be bothered again.

I was bothered during the next two administrations, but stood pat and won out. Eventually, other departments seeing that we were getting by began refusing to pay. Then both parties abolished the system.

A phase of political favoritism was defeated when a field warden apprehended a prominent attorney, with considerable political influence, fishing out of season, without a license and in possession of undersize trout. He raised a lot of hell when arrested, and made dire threats against the officer, who phoned me to come help him out. The attorney had been a friend of my father and me. After greetings he said, "This little snip thinks he can prosecute me. Why, Barker, I endorsed you for your appointment, and this is no way to treat me."

I said, "I said I appreciated your endorsement, here is a copy of your telegram which says, 'I recommend the appointment of Elliott Barker as State Game Warden because of his knowledge of game, and because I know he will enforce the game laws without fear or favor.'"

"Oh, piffle on that," he said.

I said, "I wouldn't make you out a liar for anything in the world. Come on, let's go see the judge."

The fine he had to pay hurt less than the publicity he got. Making him pay off put a needed feather in my cap.

The department during my administration never showed favoritism to anybody who violated the game and fish laws. Through the years we had to prosecute a Governor's son-in-law, a Lieutenant Governor, a Democratic party state chairman, a member of the legislature, Chief of State Police, doctors, lawyers, businessmen, a priest, preachers, and ten thousand less prominent people for violation of the game and fish laws, and we got by without reproach.

In the first years of my administration I was dismayed to see the vast array of opportunities in the field of wildlife conservation and management which could not be taken advantage of due to lack of funds. We were in the midst of the great depression and times were unbelievably hard. Revenue from hunting and fishing license fees was all we had. Not one dime was received from the general fund or other appropriation. The hundred thousand dollars a year was a pitifully small sum—one thirty-fifth of today's Department budget.

Some important aspects of wildlife conservation and management in which lack of funds thwarted our progress were: Waterfowl was at a low ebb and badly needed refuge and other habitat development; politically established trout hatcheries had to be replaced; considerable predator contol was a must if we were to build up the deer and turkey population; many more field wardens were needed, for my five district wardens could not possibly patrol the seventy-eight million-acre state adequately to enforce the game laws; bighorn sheep had been exterminated from the state and needed to be restored; elk likewise had been exterminated and had been restored only in a few places, and many more areas needed restocking. In a dry state, water development would help quail and other wildlife; pronghorn antelope were absent from three-fourths of their original habitat, and devising ways to re-establish them on their indigenous range was highly desirable.

We simply had to take first things first and bide our time to go forward with other projects and programs.

Of course we did law enforcement work

and some predator control from the outset. We very soon abandoned a politically established trout hatchery with a fifty gallons of water a minute water supply, and began development of a replacement fifteen miles distant with twenty-five hundred gallons a minute springs for the water supply. We took care of the Black Canyon deer population problem the first fall season despite emotional and sentimentalist opposition.

CHAPTER SIX

The Black Canyon Challenge

During three legislative sessions the New Mexico Game Protective Association, representing the sportsmen of the state, worked diligently for passage of legislation to invest the Game Commission with full regulatory authority to manage the wildlife and fisheries resources. One of the strong arguments for the law was that such flexibility for game management was necessary for the control of deer populations on overstocked segments of their habitat.

Yet when the Game Commission, under the new law the GPA had supported, proposed an antlerless deer season in the terribly over-populated Black Canyon area, sportsmen, including the president of the GPA, rebelled against it. Doe deer had been contraband game for so long that here seemed to be a halo over their heads. To many people, doe killing was unthinkable, despite the fact that it was the only possible way to reduce the population and prevent mass starvation of the animals.

Trapping and moving three thousand deer from the remote area was obviously impossible even if funds had been available. Yet trapping had been tried by the previous administration and failed without one deer being trapped and moved.

A basic principle of good game management is that game, such as deer and elk, must be kept within the carrying capacity of their habitat in order to preserve both the game and its habitat. The infamous case in Arizona, where forty thousand deer starved to death and their habitat was destroyed for failure to keep deer within the carrying capacity of the range, should have been lesson enough but it wasn't.

Black Canyon was an area of about a hundred square miles of ideal deer habitat in the Gila National Forest of southwest New Mexico. It had been a refuge for about ten years, and predator control, mainly for protection of livestock, had been rather intensive.

Since there were no roads into the area, it was quite difficult of access. Heavy hunting in the areas both north and south of it, which were more accessible, had caused deer to drift into the refuge. All of these factors had brought on a very serious overstocking of the range, and all browse plants were rapidly deteriorating and many had been killed. The population was estimated to be thirty-five deer per square mile.

Cattle also used the area and some reduction in numbers had been made. Cattle are mainly grazers and deer are browsers. It was significant that grass was good over the entire area, while browse plants such as mountain mahogany, fendler, gray and live oak were stripped of their leaves and annual growth twigs, causing many to die. Even pitchy pinon, juniper, young fir and often young pine trees were stripped of every needle as high as deer could reach standing on their hind legs.

It seems odd that deer will starve to death where grass is abundant, but it is a fact. Deer will eat very little grass except in the spring when the tender new growth first comes up.

In the spring of 1931 the new Game Commission and I, its executive officer, had to meet the challenge of doing what had to be done despite sportsmen's and other public sentiment against it. Positive and effective action was long overdue, and procrastination would only worsen the situation. With the

53

bristling protests and threats it was like a dog tackling a porcupine from the rear!

Despite all that, upon my recommendation, endorsed by the U.S. Forest Service, the Black Canyon Refuge was opened for hunting during the regular season of October 20 to 31 with a bag limit of two does or a buck and a doe. In our judgement, drastic reduction of the deer population was imperative in order to save the habitat and prevent mass deer starvation. Taking of bucks only could not accomplish the objective, hence, a buck without an antlerless deer was not permitted. That is, a hunter had to take a doe first, then get a buck if he could.

In view of the advance clamor against the antlerless season, we estimated that eight hundred hunters would participate, but almost twice that many took advantage of the season. Such a congestion of hunters set the stage for shooting accidents. One man was killed when his partner's rifle was accidentally discharged while they were sitting on a log in the hunting area.

The hunt was well supervised, and every hunter was checked in and out of the area. I personally had charge of the hunt, and patrolled the area widly on horseback throughout the hunting period. The evening before the season opened some of the Game Protective Associations of southwest New Mexico posted big red signs all over the central part of the area urging hunters not to kill does. Quite a number of irreconcilable sportsmen stayed, not to hunt, but to raise all the hell they could with me, members of my force and Forest Rangers who were helping patrol the area. The Rangers forced then to take down all the signs they had posted on Forest Service property.

There were 2,333 deer killed and checked out, an estimated 500 left the area during the hunt and 500 were killed and left due to poor condition, eaten in camp or spoiled.

Through the press and otherwise we were taken to task for what was termed a wanton slaughter of game in a wild, rampaging hunt. Dr. J. Stokely Ligon, a biologist and game authority of high repute, had been loaned to the Game Department by the U.S. Biological Survey (now the Bureau of Sports Fisheries and Wildlife). He had been in on some of the preseason inspections and had strongly urged drastic reduction of the deer population. Dr. Ligon said in his post season report: "After the hunt, misleading statements and reports relative to the Black Canyon deer kill were running riot. Deputy Birmingham and I carefully inspected the unit after the close of the season and found no such horrible conditions as reported. . . . Apparently a greater percent of the kill was salvaged than is ordinarily true during normal hunting seasons.

"No other plan open to the Game Department would have resulted in sufficient reduction of the herd. The situation, we feel, demanded such drastic remedy. Had a more orderly and limited number of hunters gone into the congested area under careful supervision most of the deer could have evaded them, and the necessary kill would not have resulted. The Game Department gambled on the outcome and won.

"The large percent of dry does, the fact that all deer were poor and underweight, that antlers of the bucks were small, undeveloped and often freakish, and the number of muley bucks, combined with the bad condition of the browse seems to prove that the heavy kill was justified."

For me the big lesson in wildlife conservation was: never let such a situation occur again! We never had another case as bad as that, but despite low deer population over the state as a whole, there were many local situations where antlerless deer had to be harvested.

Despite the bitterness over Black Canyon, and the fact that it put me and the Game Commission temporarily in the doghouse, it served well as a pilot example of conservation of wildlife habitat in order that it might support a normal number of deer on a sustained production basis. Had we not taken timely action as we did, there probably would have been a starvation die-off of equally as many deer, for that season was followed by the terrible drouth of the dust bowl era.

The Shelton Ranch in the Sacramento Mountains was the next unit where we had to reduce the number of deer through an antlerless season. We handled that unit a bit differently by issuing only a given number of permits each season for two or three years. Thus, the reduction was gradual. There was comparatively little opposition to those seasons. Through them, we succeeded in convincing most sportsmen that such seasons are necessary as an implement of good game management.

Our pioneer work in this phase of conservation of wildlife and its habitat not only laid the foundation for good game management in New Mexico, but provided good examples for other western states as well. I must confess that it took a lot of courage, or just plain bulldog stubbornness, to go through with the Black Canyon season in the face of the rabid opposition we had from the sportsmen, the public and some of the news media. As Dr. Ligon said, we gambled and won, and neither I nor any member of the Game Commission was fired.

57

CHAPTER SEVEN

The Battle for States' Rights Preservation

The period from 1932 to 1936 was a nightmare for the Department of Game and Fish and sportsmen. We were beset by the great depression, and the effects of the dust bowl era engulfed us. Low water in streams, some even drying up, lakes low and some drained hurt the fisheries resources terribly. There were terrific losses of livestock on the ranges, and big game suffered along with them.

For two years there was almost no quail and prairie chicken nesting, resulting in their numbers dropping exceedingly low. Prairie chicken habitat, limited to the sandy country of eastern new Mexico, was virtually destroyed. Both food and natural cover were dried out and tramped out by livestock which were unfit for market and struggling for their own existence. It became increasingly obvious that major restoration of habitat would have to be done to save the lesser prairie chickens from extinction.

New and some old homesteaders on marginal land were stricktly up against it in many areas, and they resorted to killing of wildlife for subsistence. To prosecute them was an exercise in frustration. They could not pay a fine and would have to go to jail; that simply increased the desperation of their families. How could the wardens do their duty?

The Department of Game and Fish struggled along on about a hundred thousand dollars a year. Finally, the rains came and environmental conditions improved gradually. The trend of the economic situation was back toward normal, and along with it the Department revenue began to increase. Naturally, with normal precipitation, game habitat began to improve, but so much damage had been done that the recovery process was quite slow.

In 1934 two federal actions of great importance took place—one good and one bad. The good one, primarily affecting the western public land states, was passage of the Taylor Grazing Act. This brought eighty million acres, about half of the public domain lands, not including Alaska, under administration for the purpose of regulating their use and to stop soil erosion.

The public domain lands consisted of government owned lands not set aside for specific purposes such as national forests, national parks, wildlife refuges, etc. Hitherto it had been first come first served in the free use of these lands for livestock grazing. Keen competition and overstocking had wrought great damage to the lands and reduced their carrying capacity for both livestock and game.

Wildlife administrators of the western states, sportsmen and other conservationists welcomed the act as a long overdue first step in providing for regulated use of the public lands and their restoration for the benefit of livestock and wildlife. They were greatly dismayed and disappointed that no provision whatsoever was made in the law for wildlife to share in the use of the public lands. We all foresaw battles ahead to have provisions for wildlife inserted in the regulations for land use authorized by the act. We felt that wildlife should have the right to share to a reasonable extent in the use of these lands.

The other action, completely unacceptable, was the promulgation by the Secretary of Agriculture of regulations designated as G-20-A and T-8½. Regulation G-20-A would authorize the U.S. Forest Service to assume complete control of wildlife on unlimited specified areas of national forest lands, set seasons and bag limits and issue hunting licenses all in complete disregard of States' rights in the wildlife arena. Regulation T-8½ provided penalties to be assessed for violation of provisions of game takeovers set up under regulation G-20-A.

Game administrators generally and many organizations considered this to be an initial probing step toward a takeover by the federal government of wildlife control and management which is an inherent prerogative of the several states. The Western Association of State Game and Fish Commissioners took the initiative in combating these regulations as unconstitutional, unnecessary and an intolerable infringement on States' rights.

The Western Association, consisting of the Game Departments of the eleven western states, was organized in Santa Fe, New Mexico, about 1918, and for many years had worked to improve wildlife and fisheries laws, wildlife conditions and management, and to protect states' rights. New Mexico was an active member, and upon becoming State Game Warden, I attended annual meetings in Arizona, Utah and Colorado. In 1934 the annual meeting was scheduled to be held in Portland, Oregon. These regulations were uppermost on the agenda.

61

Judge Colin Neblett, Chairman of the New Mexico Game Commission, Dr. Irvin Vining, member of the Oregon Game Commission, and Newell B. Cook, Director of the Utah Department of Game and Fish, had been appointed by the Western Association President, Frank Wire, to draft a resolution on the obnoxious regulations to present at the meeting. However, these men found that it was impossible to get together before the meeting. Therefore, due to Judge Neblett's fine reputation as a federal judge, and his strong sentiments on States' rights, the other members of the committee passed the buck to him to draft the resolution.

Judge Neblett was a busy man with a propensity to deal with principles rather than details. Therefore, he outlined the points to be covered in the highly important resolution and directed me to draft it. It was no easy undertaking. Then at the meeting he had me present it. For the benefit of those present not conversant with the provisions of the controversial regulations, I made the following statement as a preamble to the resolution:

"Regulation G-20-A, ostensibly to protect national forest lands and to provide better game management, provides that upon recommendation of the Chief Forester, the Secretary of Agriculture may, upon designated National Forests or portions thereof, establish hunting and fishing seasons, fix bag and creel limits, specify the sex of animals to be killed, charge fees for hunting and fishing permits.

"Regulation T-8½ would make it illegal to hunt for or take any game or non-game animal, or game or non-game fish, fur-bearing, or predatory animal, or game or non-game bird on any Forest so designated except under permit of the Forest Service, for which a fee is to be charged.

"The states' authority over game is ignored entirely by the regulation. No reference whatever is made to state laws or state authorities, nor to requirements for state hunting and fishing licenses. The fact that letters of instructions to forest officers indicate that the regulation is to be applied only in specific cases where cooperation of states has been unsatisfactory does not justify an illegal regulation wholly impossible of practical application."

Then I read the resolution as follows:

"Your committee appointed to study and report on Section G-20-A of the order of the Secretary of Agriculture has met and considered the said section and has heard arguments thereupon, and your committee unanimously reports as follows:

"Since the days of early England, it has been the unquestioned right of the sovereign to control the taking of fish and game. Prior to the Magna Charta, the title to fish and game was fixed in the crown and since that time, and particularly since the adoption of

63

the system of English common law by the sovereign states of the United States, it uniformly has been held that the title to fish and game within the boundaries of a state is vested in that state in trust, however, for the people thereof. This theory has been upheld uniformly by the decisions of courts of last resort in every state where the matter has had judicial cognizance; and by the Supreme Court of the United States where it has been on appeal many times. It is submitted that inasmuch as the question presented by section G-20-A here in question, already has had judicial interpretation of the courts, the states affected should take a determined stand, that these judicial decisions shall not be reversed by usurpation by any ambitious government department or bureau.

"We feel the threatened enforcement of G-20-A is an unlawful appropriation of the property of the people of a sovereign state which the officers of that state, and particularly the Fish and Game Commissions thereof are sworn to defend. Any attempt on the part of a federal bureau or agency to transgress upon this duty and right is in direct violation of all the principles of the organic acts and constitutions of the states involved as well as of the federal Constitution itself.

"It is also in direct violation of the spirit of all statutes and acts promulgated by the Congress of the United States, and of the judicial interpretations rendered thereupon. We believe the states involved should, if necessary, curb the threat before same is accepted in any part by the public, for while the initial steps toward the enforcement of this section of the order may seem mild and only inconsequential in result, still it may be the initial step in complete usurpation of States' rights amounting to confiscation of property without due process of law.

"We feel that the principle is entirely unsound, unjust and entirely uncalled for. Therefore, we respectfully recommend that all states involved unite in most strenuously resisting any attempt of the federal bureaus in effecting the menacing threats contained in said order.

"We have been and still are appreciative of any cooperative work done by the federal bureaus in cooperation with Fish and Game Commissions of the several states in furtherance of propagation and protection of wildlife, and we shall continue to welcome such cooperation so long as same does not ripen into usurpation of state powers; and to the end that States' rights be safeguarded and that any attempted usurpation might be checked at its inception, it respectfully recommends that this Association appoint an interim committee to consist of three members to be appointed from the states constituting this Association. Such committee to be appointed by the president and to devise ways and means to bring about early determination of the question herein involved. Such committee to be subject to the call of the chairman of the committee."

The resolution sets forth clearly the legal side of the question, and little remains to be said on that angle. But there were brought out equally strong arguments against it from the standpoint of the practical side of administrative application. The confusion with the Forest Service seasons and bag limits on forest lands with state seasons, bag limits and license requirements on adjacent lands and private lands within the forest would make application of G-20-A unworkable and intolerable.

The U.S Forest Service was well represented by high ranking officials and were given a chance to defend the regulation. They argued that the whole purpose was to enable the Forest Service to reduce big game on specific forests or segments of forests where the states could not or would not act to prevent overpopulation of, and damage to, the range. They became greatly embarrassed for want of a plausible answer when they were asked, "If that is so, then why were predatory animals, fur bearers, birds and fish included? Have they ever been known to overgraze or overbrowse a game range?"

After the day long discussion of G-20-A and T-8½ regulations and adoption of the committee's resolution as the position of the Western Association, I made these closing remarks: "Congress should be called upon to set by law procedures for protection of National Forests from overuse by game animals in the very rare instances where this occurs, and where cooperation cannot be secured from the state authorities. Specific cases should be dealt with by specific action applicable thereto. Certainly no justification exists for a general regulation such as G-20-A to be held as a club over state officials who are, and have been cooperating fully with the Forest Service.

"If the Forest Service has the authority claimed by G-20-A, then the states are administering the game and fish laws and regulations on the forests merely by the grace of God and passive consent of the Forest Service without any constitutional right. I cannot believe such is the case, and obviously both state and federal government cannot have administrative authority. Gentlemen, let us fight to the last ditch to retain our legal heritage to control and manage the game which we are sworn to protect."

Before leaving for Portland, the New Mexico Game Protective Association had pledged its support of our position. I believe sportsmen's organizations in the other western states had, or soon did, support the Western Association's position. We needed and appreciated their backing.

Judge Neblett had an appointment in Los Angeles, California, which required us to leave the meeting before the business session and election of officers for the ensuing year took place. Major Farley, Director of the California Department of Game and Fish, was slated to be the next president. It was California's turn, and Major Farley seemed to be a competent administrator, and had a very pleasing personality. I left my proxy vote for him and had not the slightest doubt that he would be elected.

The last thing President Wire said to me when we were ready to leave was, "Which route will you take to Los Angeles?"

"The inner route," I replied.

He said, "That will put you passing through Fresno tomorrow. Stop at the telegraph office for a telegram."

I asked why, but got no answer. Next day at Fresno I picked up the telegram and was utterly flabbergasted when I read it. It congratulated me upon being elected President of the Western Association of State Game and Fish Commissioners, and wished me luck in fighting federal usurpation of States' rights to manage wildlife.

I had not been a candidate, and I not given the possibility of being elected president a single thought. I handed Judge Neblett the wire and his grin was not altogether one of innocence.

What a responsibility! Why had they not elected Major Farley? Why should they think that I had the ability to do the job laid out for me? How could I do my regular work and take on this additional burden? My only answer as to why they had chosen me was that they knew I would have the backing and sound advice of Judge Colin Neblett.

The ensuing year was a busy one, but we made little progress in persuading the Forest Service to withdraw regulation G-20-A. The 1935 annual meeting of the Western Association was held in Santa Fe in June. Here again these federal regulations attempting to take over control of wildlife on specified National Forests occupied much of the time. We resolved to get the full cooperation of the powerful International Association of Game, Fish and Conservation Commissioners.

For the first time in the history of the Western Association it elected a man to serve a second consecutive term as President. I greatly appreciated the honor and confidence of my colleagues, but it meant another year of hard, hard long hours of work. I resolved to do my best and not let my colleagues down.

The International Association of Game, Fish and Conservation Commissioners would meet in Tulsa, Oklahoma in September, and I was requested to attend. New Mexico Department of Game and Fish was so hard up for funds that we had not paid the twenty-five dollars annual dues to the International for two years, but I would attend the meeting anyway.

CHAPTER EIGHT

Providing for Wildlife on the Public Domain

The Taylor Grazing Act, approved June 28, 1934, was the result of over forty years of endeavor to get something done to save this vast area of land from complete destruction. It was an act to stop injury to the public grazing lands by preventing overgrazing and soil deterioration; to provide for their orderly use and development; to stabilize the livestock industry dependent upon the public range, and for other purposes. So to accomplish these objectives, establishment of grazing districts was authorized.

Unfortunately, only eighty million acres

in the contiguous United States were included. Nothing was said in the Act of what would become of the remaining ninety-three million acres. Perhaps the President thought that the remainder was not worth saving, for he vetoed an amendment that would have included sixty million acres more. Many of us feared that regulating the use of only part of the public domain lands would aggravate and speed up the deterioration of the remainder.

It was, indeed, unfortunate that no provision whatsoever was made for wildlife to share in the use of these lands. Recognizing the need for specific provisions for wildlife in the rules and regulations to govern the grazing districts, the State Game Commission and I promptly initiated action to accomplish that end. At first both stockmen and the Department of Interior Officials argued that there was no need for such provisions. As head of the State Game Department and president of the Western Association of State Game and Fish Commissioners, I insisted that such provisions must be included in the grazing district rules and regulations.

The stockmen held many meetings, usually presided over by Ferry Carpenter, representing the Department of Interior, trying to come to agreement on a set of rules and regulations to govern the grazing districts. Other conservationists and I always attended those meetings and lost no opportunity to make our input for wildlife. Dr. J. Stokley Ligon was a most valuable co-worker.

Finally, there was organized a state voluntary cooperative committee to work out an acceptable wildlife plan. The committee was composed of the New Mexico Cattle Growers Association, the New Mexico Wool Growers Association, the New Mexico Game Protective Association, the State College, the University of New Mexico, the Southwest Conservation League, the Department of Game and Fish and the State Land Commissioner.

After several unproductive meetings, I presented the committee with a set of rules which I thought all interests could live with. With a few minor amendments, my proposal was approved by the committee. These rules were endorsed by the Western Association at a special meeting in Denver, Colorado, on February 14, 1935, subject to possible alterations to meet special situations in the several states. The Department of Interior adopted the plan and it is still in force. An important battle was won!

The original rule follows, but it has been revised in some respects:

"In addition to the regularly elected advisors for each grazing district established under the Taylor Grazing Act there is hereby authorized to be appointed one district advisor in each grazing district to represent wildlife and recreational resources. Such district advisor shall have the same qualifications as the elected advisors, except that he need not be an owner of livestock, and he shall be nominated by the land-use committee of the State Planning Board. The district advisor may be appointed by the Secretary of Interior in the same manner and form as the other district advisors.

"The utilization of grazing district lands by domestic livestock shall be in accord with the following fundamental principles for propagation and conservation of wildlife and other natural resources of the public domain.

(a) *Carrying capacity to provide for game.* In estimating carrying capacities of public domain ranges and in allotment of numbers of domestic stock to be grazed within any grazing district, allowance shall be made for reasonable utilization by wildlife.

(b) *Game and bird refuges.* Game refuges necessary for adequate protection and restocking of game animals and game birds may be established within any grazing district, the location and size of such refuges to be determined so far as possible in cooperation with grazing district permittees.

(c) *Areas best suited to wildlife production.* Upon such areas as may be determined by the Secretary of Interior, upon consideration of all interests involved, to be of higher value for and better adapted to production of wildlife than to domestic stock, preference

74

shall be given to such higher use.

(d) *Game animals to be limited.* If or when game animals shall become overabundant to an extent detrimental to the range and forage thereon, the state or federal laws will be invoked to limit by removal through hunting and otherwise, the game animals on such overpopulated area until a reasonable number has been attained.

(e) *Game law observation.* All permittees on a grazing district shall be required to comply with all state and federal game laws, and local officials of the Department of the Interior shall cooperate with state officials in the enforcement of state game laws and regulations.

(f) *Administration.* Provision for observance of game regulations shall be included in each grazing permit."

When I attended the annual meeting of the International Association of Game, Fish and Conservation Commissioners in Tulsa, Oklahoma, on August 31 and September 1, 1935, the Taylor Grazing Act, as it would affect restoration of abused lands and wildlife, was foremost on the agenda. The foregoing rules came in for close scrutiny.

I had been invited to present a paper on the subject from the standpoint of a wildlife administrator and conservationist. Captain B. C. Mossman, a prominent sheep rancher, was asked to present the position of the livestock industry. Captain Mossman had been Captain of the Arizona Rangers, organized in the early 1900's to break up a big band of desperate outlaws, and he and his dozen Rangers got the job done. He was a rugged character and forceful speaker. While he and I often differed on wildlife subjects, we were very good friends.

Two days before the meeting he called me up by phone and said that something had come up to prevent him from going to the meeting. I told him I'd be glad to take his paper. He said he had prepared no paper but had planned to give a "free-wheeling talk off my sheep-smelling cuff." I knew he was capable of doing that. Then I suggested that he get some other rancher to take his place, but he said it was too late to do that. Then he said, "Barker, you go ahead and wear two hats. You know what our position is as well as I do. I'll trust you to present our view fairly."

The New Mexico Game Protective Association was unable to send a delegate to the meeting and had asked me to represent the organized sportsmen. Thus, it was that I went to the meeting wearing three hats— a game warden's, a sheepman's and a sportsman's.

After I had delivered my comprehensive talk, I was plied with questions for two solid hours. Among the interested questioners were conservation stalwarts, Seth Gordon, Secretary of the American Game Association, T. Gilbert Pearson, President of the Audubon Society, Dave Madsen, E. Lee LeCompte, Arthur Foran and others. At long last I believe that all were convinced that the plan providing for wildlife on the public domain developed by New Mexico was adequate, or at least the best that we could hope to obtain.

There were also some heated discussions of differences the New Mexico Department of Game and Fish had had with J. N. Darling, the new head of the U.S. Biological Survey, over actions he had taken without consulting the New Mexico authorities. A sample was his recommendation for setting aside a huge federal refuge on public domain lands for preservation of fantail deer (Odocoileus Couesi) less than a tenth of which was fantail deer habitat. Things like that were embarrassing our relations with the stockmen.

I was greatly disappointed that the delegates to this meeting took little interest in Forest Service regulation G-20-A, and adopted no resolution opposing it as the Western Association had. I wondered how I could explain to the Western Association why I had failed to get the International Association's support as I had promised. But there was a great surprise coming whereby that objective might soon be accomplished.

When the nominating committee, headed

by my long-time friend, Bill Tucker, head of the Texas Game Department, called me in and inquired whether or not I would accept the office of President of the great International Association of Game, Fish and Conservation Commissioners. I was completely flabbergasted! I knew it was traditional for the vice president to be elected president.

"Why not vice president, John L. Farley?" I asked.

"Because he is no longer with the California Department," Tucker said. "Also second vice president, William Reinhart, of Ohio, has left the Ohio Department."

I said, "I can't accept the position because I am too busy with my job and being President of the Western Association. Besides I am not eligible, for I am not even a member. New Mexico has not been able to pay its membership dues for two years."

Then my good friend, Ray P. Holland, Editor of *Field and Stream*, and International Association Treasurer, spoke up and said, "You are wrong, Elliott, New Mexico's dues are paid and you are a bona fide member."

I said, "No, Ray, that is not so. I know we haven't paid up."

The Treasurer then produced his books which showed that New Mexico's dues had been paid. Tears came to my eyes when I realized that my friend, Ray Holland, had understood our dire financial situation due to the depression and the dust bowl drouth, and had magnanimously paid the dues out of his own pocket. What a wonderful friend!

I then aruged that it would be too burdensome to perform the duties of president of both the Western and International Associations and at the same time do justice to my position of State Game Warden. Bill Tucker said, "Any man who can come here wearing three hats and represent the New Mexico Department of Game and Fish, the organized sportsmen and the cattle and sheep men, can continue to wear three hats. We are going to nominate and elect you and we want you to serve."

It was, indeed, a great honor. I am the only man ever to hold the office of president of both of these great organizations at the same time, except Harry Woodward, of Colorado, who two years ago, held both offices for a couple of months.

I was so busy during the ensuing year that I can hardly remember what happened. For one thing, I was one of the midwives at the birth of the National Wildlife Federation which will be dealt with in the next chapter. I did get the International Association interested in Forest Service regulation G-20-A and T-8½, but I fell short of getting the regulations withdrawn during my tenure as President of the International.

A short while after my tenure expired, as

a result of the efforts of these organizations and others the regulations were replaced by satisfactory cooperative regulations. From that time on States' rights to manage wildlife and the Forest Service's duty to manage its habitat on the National Forests have been recognized as proper and constitutional division of jurisdiction between the states and federal government.

The 1936 meeting of the International Association was held in Grand Rapids, Michigan. I shall not go into what took place there except as to the choice of the 1937 meeting place. Meetings had been held in Canada, but not in Mexico despite the fact that the Republic of Mexico had long been a member of the organization. So Bill Tucker, of Texas, I. T. Quinn, of Alabama, and I staged a campaign to take the 1937 meeting to Mexico City. We had a hard time selling the idea, especially to the American Fisheries Society which traditionally had held its meetings at the same place, just before or after the International. We finally were successful in converting a majority.

After the formalities of the first session in Mexico City, I was scheduled to give an important address. Only a handful of our three hundred registered were present. The others were scouting the interesting city. Out of courtesy about a hundred and fifty Mexicans were present in the great Hall of Fine

Arts. Everyone was surprised when I discarded my prepared speech and addressed the audience in Spanish on general wildlife topics for fifteen minutes. Never have I received such applause!

Another surprising thing happened. When my wife, thirteen-year old daughter and I registered at the Reforma Hotel and were escorted to our room we found it to be a plush three-room suite, the finest in the hotel. I rushed back down to the registration desk and told the clerk that I had reserved only a room with two beds, and that I could not afford the suite to which they had assigned me.

He said, "Oh yes, you can."

I said, "No, I can't. Please change us to the kind of room I reserved."

"No, Mr. Barker," the affable, English-speaking, clerk said. "You were the one who brought these big conventions here, and this suite is being provided to you free of any charge to show our appreciation." Can you beat that for gratitude and hospitality?

I certainly did not do anything of outstanding importance while I was President of the International. I worked hard to keep its programs going, memberships up and perhaps took the leadership in a few things and tried to put on a good convention in Grand Rapids. However, twenty-eight years later it seems that some of the old-timers must have remembered my leadership, when similar problems came up, for they sent me a fine gold-plated plaque on a 12 by 16-inch frame which has this inscription: IN RECOGNITION OF ELLIOTT S. BARKER FOR HIS SERVICES AS PRESIDENT OF THE INTERNATIONAL ASSOCIATION OF GAME, FISH AND CONSERVATION COMMISSIONERS 1936.

*The author at 89 still directs 10-day Wilderness
Trail Rides.*
Photo: Santa Fe, NEW MEXICAN.

Photos are by author or members of his family unless
otherwise noted.

Top: The author and Ethel, his wife of 65 years, reviewing books. Bottom: Pecos Wilderness Trail Riders.

Top: Mule deer buck, antlers in velvet. Bottom: A glimpse of desert bighorn sheep in Hatchet Mountains.

Top: Destructive over-browsing by deer in Black Canyon. Bottom: Sheep grazing in high country.

Top: Juniper defoliated as high as deer can reach standing on hind legs. Bottom: Common sight in Dust Bowl era.

Top: Restocking of beavers resulted in many beautiful dams and ponds. Bottom: New Mexico's big trout hatchery.

Top: 75 years ago this burned forest greatly impressed the author. Bottom: Sample of wasteful soil erosion.
Top Photo: Very old, unknown.

Top: Burn where Smokey was rescued.
Bottom Left: Smokey recuperating (enlarged).
Bottom Right: Smokey ready for trip to his
new home in Washington Zoo.
Photos: Harold Walter.

Top: Barbary sheep in truck enroute to new home on open range. Bottom: Fine Merriam wild turkeys.

Top: Sportsman-built Truchas Lake Dam. Bottom: Lovely Truchas Lake deepened by sportsmen—a good local club project.

Top: Antelope trapping was successful.
Bottom: Elk, exterminated from New Mexico
have been restocked and are thriving.
Bottom Photo: Department of Game and Fish.

Smokey Bear, world famous animal, in his deluxe quarters in the National Zoo. He is now 26 years old and has been retired. Photo: U.S. Forest Service.

CHAPTER NINE

The National Wildlife Federation

February 3 to 7, 1936, will go down in history as the birthday of an era in wildlife and related natural resource conservation and management. President Franklin Delano Roosevelt called the First National Wildlife Conference to convene on those dates. In calling this conference, the President said:

"My purpose is to bring together individuals, organizations and agencies interested in the restoration and conservation of wildlife resources. My hope is that through this conference new cooperation between public and private interests, and between

Canada, Mexico and this country will be developed; that from it will come constructive proposals for concrete action; that through these proposals existing state and federal government agencies and conservation groups can work cooperatively for the common good."

Chief Forester, F. A. Silcox, was appointed chairman of the conference committee, with ex officio members, Harold Ickes, Secretary of the Interior, Daniel C. Roper, Secretary of Commerce and Henry A. Wallace, Secretary of Agriculture. The President appointed the following committee to organize, promote and set up the meeting:

Elliott S. Barker, New Mexico; Frank T. Bell, U.S. Bureau of Fisheries; Arno B. Cammerer, National Park Service; Charles E. Clark, Jr., Florida; Powel Grosley, Jr., Ohio; J. N. Darling, Iowa; Wm. L. Finley, Oregon; Ira N. Gabrielson, Chief U.S. Biological Survey; H. S. Graves, Connecticut; John A. Hartwell, New York; J. K. Kinnear, Ohio; Mrs. Roberta C. Lawson, Oklahoma; E. S. Martin, New York; David C. Mills, Connecticut; Nathan Moran, California; Frank E. M. Mullen, New York; Edward A. O'Neal, Alabama; I. T. Quinn, Alabama; Kermit Roosevelt, New York; L. J. Tabor, Ohio; C. A. Wheatly, Texas, and George W. Wood, Iowa.

While Carl D. Shoemaker, Secretary of the Senate Special Committee on Wildlife Resources, was not on the Committee he

84

rendered yeoman service. I felt deeply honored by being named to the Committee, but the distance from New Mexico to Washington, D. C. made it difficult for me to be of much assistance. I did the best I could by correspondence and a couple of phone calls. I was asked to present a talk on *Game Management By Public Agencies.*

Response to the President's call was excellent. Some fifteen hundred delegates from all over the United States, Canada and Mexico attended. From the outset it was apparent that the delegates had come for business and meant to get results. Philanthropist, Arthur N. Pack, and rancher, G. W. Evans accompanied me from New Mexico.

It is impossible to give more than the briefest sketch of what took place. There were seven general sessions and twelve special sessions. There were six related meetings, including one of the International Association of Game, Fish and Conservation Commissioners, of which I was president. The book of proceedings of the conference has 370,000 words and 77 page and half-page photographic illustrations.

The topic of the first session, after opening formalities, was on: *The Wild Life Crisis.* Topics of other general sessions were: *Why Concern Ourselves With Wildlife?, The Status of Wildlife, The Solutions of Wildlife Problems by Education and Management* involved two

85

sessions, at one of which, I delivered my paper on *Wildlife Management by Public Agencies.* This gave me the opportunity to present our problem with the U.S. Forest Service involving regulation G-20-A and T-8½. The final general session topic was *A North American Program for Wildlife Restoration.*

I presided at that session. The day and night before there had been a terrific snow storm piling the snow sixteen inches deep. Traffic was stalled, and it was impossible to get a taxi. Hence the attendance was disappointing. In my opening remarks I said, "I am very sorry that this snow storm has made the attendance much smaller than we expected. I believe our topic gets to the heart of this whole convention. A general program for wildlife restoration is what we came here to talk about, and more important, to do something about. Our first speaker this morning needs no introduction to any conservation audience. It is not necessary for me to eulogize his conservation attributes because they are too well known. It gives me great pleasure to present the Congressman from Virginia, the Honorable A. Willis Robertson."

The Congressman made a wonderfully interesting and effective talk. I wish there were space to present it here. To illustrate some of the unanswerable questions about wildlife he told this story: It seems an old, Black preacher was preaching about the creation and said, "God created the heavens and the earth, and he said, 'Let there be light,' and there was light; and then God created the land, and the trees and the flowers and the birds. But God wasn't satisfied, he wanted a man. God made the first man and named him Adam. He made Adam out of mud and set him up agin the fence to dry."

A brother back in the audience said, "Parson, you said Adam was the first man?"

"Yes brother, he was."

"And God made him out of mud and set him up agin the fence to dry?"

"Yes brother, that's shore right."

"Parson," the brother asked, "who made that fence?"

The parson said, "Brother, them's the kind of questions that hurts religion."

There were several other interesting and informative speakers on that morning's program. When the session adjourned it was the end of the historic wildlife conference. I believe everyone felt that a great deal had been accomplished. Now we would have to go back home and sell the programs agreed upon to our people and conservation organizations.

The special sessions previously referred to were on such topics as: Farmer-Sportsmen's Cooperatives, Fish Management, Upland Wildlife Research, Game Breeding, Forests and Forest Wildlife, Stream and Lake Improvement, Wildlife Disease and Populations Cycles Research, Research in Waterfowl Problems, Pollution, Practical Wildlife Management, The Problem of Vanishing Species, etc.

There were many prominent and powerful speakers at both the regular and special sessions. Among them were, Seth Gordon, Dr. Aldo Leopold, Dr. Ira N. Gabrielson, Senator Key Pitmann and others.

Mr. J. N. Darling, of Iowa, who for a short time before had served as Chief of the U.S. Biological Survey, had been selected by the conference committee to serve as Chairman of the Organization Committee. I believe Thomas Beck and Aldo Leopold were the other members of the Committee. The third day of the conference was set aside for a report of the Organization Committee and its subcommittees in an effort to form a workable national organization. Mr. Darling presided at this session.

In his opening remarks Mr. Darling emphasized that this meeting and its results were not designed to favor any particular interests, or state or federal departments. He said, "It is my duty and privilege to attempt an amalgamation of all conservation factions into a national working unit, or outline a method which may accomplish that amalgamation."

He highly complimented a young man representing the Junior Chamber of Commerce upon a talk he had given on the need for a

National Wildlife Federation. The Chairman presented several other speakers who made some brief remarks. One was Mr. Lythgo Osborne, of New York, who predicted that a National Wildlife Organization would be formed, and warned that troubles were sure to be encountered and have to be overcome. He said one thing we must do was to stop warfare among ourselves.

In his final remarks, before we got down to the business of organizaing, Chairman Darling said, "We may best approach the subject of a National Wildlife Federation by reviewing the processes by which we arrived at the present set up for a Federation. . . . I want to make it clear that if wildlife conservation is to succeed, the demands must come from the individual voter to your elected government officials by word of mouth, by letter or by wire."

Senator Fredrick C. Wolcott made a last minute plea for formation of a National Wildlife Organization. He said, "I should like to see a broad platform that will start an organization today, that will insist upon regional treatment and that will not wait for a whole year before we tackle it again as a permanent organization."

At long last, Mr. Paul O. Peters of Missouri, made this historic motion: "I move that it is the sense of this meeting that an organization be formed as outlined by Mr. Darling." The

89

motion was seconded by several members. There were no objections nor discussions. The vote was unanimous in favor of organizing a National Wildlife Federation. The long endured labor pains were terminating in fruition! Mr. Colin N. Reed, of Pennsylvania, nominated Mr. J. N. Darling for Chairman. The nomination was seconded and Mr. Seth Gordon took the chair and put the motion to a vote. Again the motion was adopted unanimously, followed by tremendous applause.

Mr. Darling's acceptance comments were brief and to the point. He called a conference of the working organization committees which had been appointed to draft a proposal for a constitution, and dismissed the remainder of the audience until 2:30 that afternoon.

Upon convening at 2:30, the proposed constitution for a Wildlife Organization was presented for consideration. It was read to the audience by Carl D. Shoemaker. Copies had been distributed.

The proposed name of the organization was, General Wildlife Federation. Thirteen regions had been set up each to elect one director, and these thirteen directors were to be the governing body of the organization. The list of the first board of directors follows: Region 1., F. C. Wolcott, Connecticut; Region 2., N. Marks Bump, New York; Region 3., A. C. Hayward, North Carolina; Region 4., I. T. Quinn, Alabama; Region 5., Kenneth

Taylor, Kentucky; Region 6., L. A. Colby, Illinois; Region 7., W. J. P. Aberg, Wisconsin; Region 8., Wm. J. Tucker, Texas; Region 9., Frank J. Brady, Nebraska; Region 10., Elliott S. Barker, New Mexico; Region 11., Wm. T. Finley, Oregon; Region 12., Joseph S. Dixon, California; Region 13., G. W. Grebe, Idaho. These names are listed on a plaque in the fine National Wildlife Federation headquarters building, 1412, 16th Street NW., Washington, D. C..

Article II of the constitution set forth the objectives of the federation as follows: "The Purposes of the Federation are:

(a) To organize all agencies, societies, clubs and individuals which are, or should be, interested in the restoration and conservation of wildlife into a permanent, unified agency for the purpose of securing adequate public recognition of the needs and the values of wildlife resources.

(b) To develop a comprehensive program for the advancement, restoration and conservation of wildlife.

(c) To present to the public such pertinent facts, discoveries and information as may contribute to the solution of the problems involved in the restoration and conservation of wildlife.

(d) To cooperate with other general wildlife federations in other countries on this continent."

91

There seems to be no need to burden the reader with the rather lengthy remaining eleven articles of the constitution. The tentative constitution was adopted, but to become permanent it would have to be ratified by the states just as the United States Constitution was. Naturally through the years there were to be some amendments and changes, but the basis was sound and was ratified by the states.

Upon adoption of the tentative contitution, J. N. Darling was nominated and elected unanimously as president of the General Wildlife Federation. Fredrick C. Wolcott was elected first vice president, I. T. Quinn second vice president and Wm. L. Finley, third vice president. The objectives of the conference had been accomplished.

President Darling then took the chair and thanked the delegates for their confidence in his ability to serve them. His first official act was to appoint a committee on international relations. Delegates from both Canada and Mexico had participated in the conference. He named Alonzo Stewart, from the United States, Mr. J. W. Harkins, of Canada and Señor Juan Zinzer from Mexico.

President Darling then said, "We have in our midst men who have worked incessantly toward the accomplishment of the aims and ends which we have sought and accomplished today. I would like to call on some of them."

He first presented Mr. Thomas Beck, who

had served on the organization committee with him. Mr. Beck made a short, inspiring statement and praised Mr. Darling and the delegates for the success of the meeting. Next, Mr. John Baker of the Audubon Society was called upon and he pledged the full cooperation of the Society.

I was seated in the very back row of seats in the great hall beside my friend of twenty-four years, Dr. Aldo Leopold. I fully expected him to be called upon, and Mr. Darling called upon him next, with high praise for his contribution to the success of the conference. Dr. Leopold went to the platform and made some constructive comments and gave a bit of sound advice. He was applauded enthusiastically. (For some unknown reason the foregoing item was omitted from the proceedings record, but it occurred as stated.)

Injection of a sidelight here seems appropriate. Both G. W. Evans and I had come to Washington dressed in our best western garb, including high-heeled cowboy boots, and had come in for some friendly ribbing. When I registered at the Mayflower Hotel I was greeted in the lobby by a few friends who had arrived early, then I was escorted to my room. Soon the phone rang and I was asked if my room was all right. I said, "Yes it seems to be," and hung up.

In a couple of minutes there was a second call and the voice said, "Are you sure your room is satisfactory, and have you found everything you need?"

I said, "Certainly, who is this and why so inquisitive?"

The reply was, "I'm the bell captain, and we wanted to be sure you had found a place to keep your horse."

As Dr. Leopold returned to his seat, I was greatly surprised when President Darling said, "This is going to be mean on this fellow. He won't like it, but I am going to call on him anyway. He is President of the International Association of Game, Fish and Conservation Commissioners. Elliott Barker of New Mexico."

My Alabama friend, I. T. Quinn, rose and said, "He is not only President of the International, but of the Western Association of State Game and Fish Commissioners as well."

As I self-consciously clumped up the long isle in my cowboy boots, Mr. Quinn came to meet me and escorted me to the podium amidst friendly applause.

The proceedings record shows I said:

"The President has been most unfair I think, in calling upon a man of my limited abilities as a public speaker to make any remarks extemporaneously.

"I just want to say one thing, that to my mind, if all the words uttered annually on behalf of conservation and if all the resolutions that are passed at the various conventions that are held as wildlife conservation conven-

94

tions, could be converted into real, effective action for the benefit of wildlife, there would be a decidedly different picture of wildlife over the country today.

"If this tentative organization that has been set up here today, for ratification by our people back in the states, only serves as a means to produce more words and more resolutions, it will have failed dismally. What we need is more action, more direct action, more getting the job done. Unless this new organization, or federation, can serve that purpose, then I can see no good in it.

"I sincerely hope that it will be a success. I can see a great many troubles ahead, but I hope we can make it a success, that we can all cooperate and make it go. I, personally, am going to do all that I can to make it successful out in our western country. But if we do not operate on the basis of actually getting action instead of more words and resolutions, then all of our efforts will have been in vain."

"I thank you." (applause)

There were a few other brief talks, and a resolution adopted thanking President Roosevelt for his foresight in calling the conference and cooperation in making it a success. Then the meeting adjourned. Thus, the great National Wildlife Federation was born. Of course it was still in its swaddling clothes, and had to have its diapers changed once in a while, and it experienced growing pains. But I am sure that no one imagined then that it would become the giant it is today.

Back at home I saw to it that the New Mexico Game Protective Association (now the New Mexico Wildlife Federation) became the state affiliate of the National Wildlife Federation. The State Game Commission and Department of Game and Fish from the outset cooperated with the National Wildlife Federation in every way possible to make it a success.

After retiring as State Game Warden in 1953, I served eight years (1959-1967) as State Representative and also as Secretary of the New Mexico Wildlife Federation. In 1960, when Earnest Swift, long-time Executive Director of the National Wildlife Federation, had to retire for health reasons, the N.W.F. Board of Directors was seeking a new Director and preferred having a man from the public land states.

A board member, Dr. Hugh B. Woodward, asked me who I would recommend. I told him that Phil Snyder, Director of the Oregon Department, or Thomas L. Kimball, Director of the Colorado Department was capable of filling the position. Mr. Snyder was not interested in it, and the position was offered to Mr. Kimball, and he accepted. He is now Executive Vice President. In his fourteen years tenure he has accomplished wonders and done a marvelous job.

The financial rate of growth during his

tenure has been 940 percent. The affiliate membership is now almost a million and a half. This group plus those citizens who join the Federation directly as associate members, and other supporting the National Wildlife Federation total an estimated three and a half million persons. The Federation's principal communication media are *National Wildlife Magazine, International Wildlife, Ranger Rick's Nature Magazine, Conservation News* and *Conservation Report.*

On March 28-31, 1974, Mrs. Barker and I attended the annual meeting of the National Wildlife Federation in Denver and enjoyed one of the best and most constructive programs we had ever heard. I was privileged to sit for a half day with the State Representatives as the alternate Representative of New Mexico. It seemed like old times.

There were over 900 registered for the meeting and over 800 attended the fabulous banquet. The arrangements for the meeting were appropriate and highly impressive. It all made me very proud to have been one of the midwives at the birth of this Wildlife Conservation Organization giant.

I am also very proud to have been awarded in 1964 the National Wildlife Federation's Bald Eagle trophy as State Conservationist of the Year, and in 1965, its Communications Conservationist Cougar Trophy.

CHAPTER TEN

Game Bird Restoration and Conservation

All of my time and efforts during the twenty-two years (1931-1953) that I was head of the New Mexico Department of Game and Fish were devoted directly, or indirectly, to wildlife restoration, conservation and management. The full story of the problems, disappointments and accomplishments during that period would fill a big, fat book. Hence, they can only be skimmed over in these pages.

Our ever present, big problem was lack of adequate finances. The Department never has received any appropriation from the general fund, but is supported entirely by revenue from hunting and fishing licenses, permit fees and miscellaneous related revenue. For the first three years of my administration the revenue was about a hundred thousand dollars a year. Then it gradually increased to about seven hundred fifty thousand at the end of my tenure in 1953. These were pitiful amounts compared with the need and the Department's budget of nearly four million dollars today.

Other problems were the dust bowl era and subsequent recurring drouths and hard winters. An annoying problem was the biennial task of preventing passage of legislation adverse to the interests of wildlife and the Department. Securing needed legislation, both state and federal, was equally annoying and time consuming. Miraculously, despite many setbacks we surmounted these problems.

During 1933 and 1934 the drouth throughout the state was severe. In the east half, particularly in the northeast quarter of the state, fields were blown out to the hardpan subsoil. Topsoil was swept away and carried all the way to the east coast. Sand drifts covered fences and piled up high against barns and dwellings. Most of the homesteaders had to move away and abandon their homes. Many of the large livestock operators shipped their livestock to pastures in other states and Mexico, but thousands of cattle and sheep, especially those of small owners, perished from starvation.

With these conditions prevailing, one can easily imagine their effect on wildlife. Deer in the mountain areas did not suffer too much, except that the fawn survival was limited. Antelope suffered some loss of adults, and for two years in the eastern half of the state the fawn crop was virtually all lost. It was certainly a severe setback.

Scaled quail in most of the state had no successful nesting for two years, and their numbers were reduced to a minimum. When rains came again in 1935 and 1936 the scaled quail recovered more rapidly than we had dared to hope. There were some areas in the state where the quail were not so hard hit, and as they became more abundant considerable trapping and transplanting to areas needing it most was done.

The lesser prairie chickens, inhabiting only the sandy country of eastern New Mexico, were decimated worse than quail. Their habitat was destroyed by drouth and overgrazing by starving livestock until they were on the verge of extermination. It seemed that if prairie chickens were to be restored, and to forestall repetition of such a tragedy, considerable areas of land would have to be acquired, fenced, water developed and their habitat restored and maintained in units distributed well over their range.

With the advent of the Federal Aid to Wildlife Act in 1939, land acquisition began,

100

and was continued for quite a number of years. We felt that units of one to two sections (square miles) here and there over their habitat would be more beneficial in restoring and maintaining the prairie chicken population than a single very large area. Grazing was eliminated and the native grasses, herbs and the dwarf havaard oak gradually came back to provide a natural habitat again. In some cases head feeds such as sorghum and milo maize was planted to supplement the natural food supply. Where well water was not available we installed rain catchment units.

In all we acquired and developed some thirty thousand acres in many units. All of this aided in restoring prairie chicken populations and insures some nesting habitat in dry years. With the chickens back in harvestable numbers, hunting seasons with low bag limits are now annually enjoyed by many sportsmen. Incidentally, both scaled and bobwhite quail and many species of non-game birds have been greatly benefited.

In the initial stages of this great restoration project, Dr. J. Stokley Ligon had a leading part. Later one of my other men, Mr. Paul Russell had charge of the project. Both men are to be given much credit for good planning and jobs well done.

We trapped some prairie chickens and stocked them in noncontiguous indigenous habitats, but they were unsuccessful. Perhaps

101

it was because heavy use of the areas by live-stock had eliminated some of the ingredients essential to their environment.

Sage chickens, which were indigenous to the sagebrush (*artemisia tridentata*) country of northwest New Mexico, were exterminated in the early 1900's. The cause may have been overshooting to some extent (there were no game laws then) but more likely the cause was overgrazing by sheep. At any rate, in 1941 I arranged with the Game and Fish Department of Wyoming to exchange some Merriam wild turkeys for sage hens on a one to two basis.

Dr. J. Stokley Ligon, an expert bird trapper, trapped the turkeys and delivered them to Wyoming, trapped forty-eight sage chickens and brought them back to New Mexico. They were released in three areas which seemed to us to have good conditions for their survival. Then later on we secured some more sage chickens and stocked them in one of the same areas. They survived for a few years and then gradually faded away until it is doubtful if any survive today. That was a great disappointment, for there are vast areas of sagebrush country available.

On the other hand, according to my last information, the Merriam turkeys, not indigenous to Wyoming, have thrived there in a number of places. So the venture was fifty percent successful.

I had Dr. Ligon do quite a lot of turkey trapping in areas of plenty to stock areas of the state where they had been depleted by one cause or another. These plantings were, for the most part, highly successful.

Another bird restoration project we undertook was to re-establish masked bobwhite quail, which had been exterminated from their limited indigenous habitat of extreme southwest New Mexico and southeast Arizona. The only source of supply was in the adjacent Republic of Mexico.

The trapping was difficult but successful. In 1938 fifty of the rare birds were secured. A few pairs were retained by Dr. Ligon for breeding in captivity, and a few pairs were given to Arizona. The remainder were released in the best available place in their native habitat. Then in 1940 twenty more were secured to supplement the original planting. It was most disappointing that the birds gradually faded away. I believe that the New Mexico and Arizona Game Departments are again trying to re-establish these rare, beautiful quail in their native habitat.

When I became State Game Warden I found that there were a number of waterfowl refuges being maintained on privately owned lands and waters where all hunting was prohibited. But there had been no development to benefit the birds. At one place on the Rio Grande the Department had acquired a few small tracts in the La Joya marshes to develop for waterflow habitat. The lands acquired included only a very small portion of the marshes. The lands had once been farm land, but siltation of the Rio Grande had raised the water table until their value for farming had been destroyed, and made them highly suitable for waterfowl marsh development.

When I went to Washington D. C. to attend the First National Wildlife Conference I had agreed with the New Mexico Game Protective Association to promote acquisition by state and federal agencies six units for waterfowl development. They were: The La Joya Marshes; the Bosque del Apache Marshes several miles down stream from La Joya; the Bitter Lakes near Roswell; Wagon Mound Lake forty miles north of Las Vegas, N.M.; Black Lakes thirty miles east and a bit south of Taos, and San Simon Marshes in the extreme southwest corner of the state.

Working with the U.S. Biological Survey we got that federal agency to acquire and develop Bosque del Apache and Bitter Lakes. They have both been made into marvelous waterfowl areas. The New Mexico Game Department went ahead and acquired and developed La Joya Marshes and made of it a very fine waterfowl area. Acquisition of some thirty small tracts was a difficult, tedious job but we finally completed it.

The Department of Game and Fish purchased Wagon Mound Lake which was once an outstanding goose resting area. Then dry farming was abandoned in the area and geese ceased to use the lake to any extent, but it is a valuable asset. San Simon Marsh is under management of the Bureau of Land Management and serves a useful purpose for the endangered New Mexico duck. However, complications with private lands in the area limit its value.

So it is that of the six areas that I promoted at the 1936 meeting in Washington, D. C. for conservation of waterfowl, five are devoted to that purpose. Black Lake alone could not be purchased.

CHAPTER ELEVEN

Restoration of Exterminated Wildlife Species

When the Pilgrim Fathers were landing on the bleak New England coast, Don Juan de Eulate was serving as the fifth governor of the Spanish Province of New Mexico. This land of enchantment was explored first in 1540-1542 by Coronado's expedition, and settled by Don Juan de Oñate's colonists in 1598. The Spanish rule continued until 1822 when Mexico obtained its freedom. It then became a Province of the Republic of Mexico. In 1846, under the treaty of Guadalupe Hidalgo, New Mexico became a territory of the United States, and gained statehood in 1912.

Throughout that period, wildlife contributed much to the subsistence of both the Indians and the invaders. However, improvident use of wildlife from 1850 to the turn of the century was disastrous to many species. Buffalo were exterminated from the area. Merriam elk, a unique subspecies indigenous to southern New Mexico and Arizona, were extirpated without even a good museum specimen being left.

The northern elk, which had inhabited all the mountain areas in the north half of the state, were wiped out completely by market hunters by about 1890. The last Rocky Mountain bighorn sheep was killed in 1902. By 1916 pronghorn antelope, which is estimated to have originally numbered near two hundred thousand, were reduced to seventeen hundred in thirty-five small bands. The last grizzly bear, unfortunately incompatible with livestock, was killed in 1930.

There still may be a question as to which came first, the chicken or the egg, but where wildlife has been exterminated from a state there can be no question about restoration coming before conservation, or is it that conservation includes restoration? Anyway, restoration went hand in hand with conservation throughout my tenure as State Game Warden.

My first restoration project was to try to re-establish Rocky Mountain bighorns in the timberline country of what is now the Pecos

107

Wilderness Area northeast of Santa Fe. It was there that the last bighorn was killed at Lake Katherine on the east side of Santa Fe Baldy. It was difficult in those days to find a source of supply for restocking.

Finally, the Superintendent of Banff National Park, Alberta, Canada, agreed to let us have six head. Two rams and four ewes were shipped in separate crates by Railway Express to Albuquerque and trucked to Santa Fe in the early spring of 1932. Snow was too deep to release them, so we built pens at the base of the mountain and fed them there until April. When released they took off for the high country of Pecos Baldy and Truchas Peaks. There they took up their abode and were seen several times over a two-year period, and then mysteriously disappeared.

We never knew what happened to them. Reports that they had been shot could not be confirmed. Domestic sheep were being summer-grazed in the area and we suspected that the bighorns had contracted disease or become infested by parasites carried by domestic animals. We felt that it was not worthwhile to try again as long as domestic sheep were being grazed in the area.

About seven years ago the situation had changed and the Department of Game and Fish obtained fifteen bighorns from Banff National Park and nine from another source and stocked them in that same country.

108

This time the plant was successful. The herd now numbers from a hundred-forty to a hundred-eighty head. They have become a great attraction for Wilderness Trail Riders and the many other users of the wilderness.

In 1939, 1940 and 1941 I obtained each year a ram and two ewes from Banff, and stocked them in the rugged Sandia Mountains just northeast of Albuquerque. The plantings took hold and developed quickly into a thriving herd of which I am very proud. Limited permit seasons for old, mature rams have been held for quite a number of years, and the spectacular animals are seen by thousands of people each year. Their esthetic value is inestimable. Not only that, but twenty-two head were trapped and transferred to the Gila Wilderness Area to establish a new herd there. Also nine head were trapped and planted in the Pecos Wilderness to supplement those from Canada. So my Sandia Mountains stocking has paid dividends in many directions.

When I became State Game Warden, elk had been reintroduced in four places by ranchers, and in one place, the Pecos Wilderness, by the Game Department. From those early plantings elk drifted out onto adjacent private and public lands in their native habitat. However, there were still many suitable range units that had no elk. As funds would permit I endeavored to stock them in those areas. Some elk were obtained from Wyoming, some

109

from Wichita Game Preserve in Oklahoma and some were trapped on the Philmont Boy Scout Ranch where there was a surplus.

We made plantings on Mount Taylor, in the Jemez Mountains and in the Carson National Forest in the Hopewell and Tres Piedras country, all of which were highly successful. Those areas as well as those stocked earlier annually provide a lot of good hunting. In the Chama country, mainly on private lands, elk have drifted in from Colorado and well stocked the country. In recent years the Department stocked other areas.

After I retired, while doing some land planning studies for the owner of a ninety-two thousand-acre mountain area, I recommended the stocking of elk to enhance the wildlife resources and land value. The owner, Mr. R. N. Round, gave me a check for a thousand dollars and said, "Get as many elk as you can with that." With it the Department of Game and Fish obtained twenty-two elk from Wyoming and planted them there to start a thriving herd.

Beavers were exterminated from the Pecos River watershed and certain other streams by early-day mountain men. Fortunately, there was an adequate supply of beavers in other areas to supply animals for trapping and transplanting. I immediately initiated a program of beaver restoration. It was neither a difficult nor expensive project. On the first planting in 1932, I personally helped pack six beavers in specially made boxes on pack horse deep into the Pecos Wilderness.

We dug out a den for them deep under a creek bank, and felled an aspen tree across the creek below the den and piled in a lot of spruce boughs to make a start on a pond for them. While we were eating our lunch the beavers came out of the improvised den and cleaned their fur at the edge of the pond. One of the adults swam down to the brush dam and inspected it thoroughly. Our inspection a couple of weeks later revealed that they had pitched in and finished the brush dam, and then gone to an off-stream marsh and started another dam below a spring. This first planting developed into a big colony which spread up and downstream for a considerable distance.

In a few years we had beavers in all suitable habitats throughout the state. Their dams made ponds which increased the trout fishing resources and enhanced the attractiveness of the mountain streams. Also the ponds, to some extent, retard sudden high waters and tend to desilt the muddy flood waters.

Beavers are very beneficial in the mountain country, but when they drift downstream into farming country they become an intolerable nuisance. They cut down fruit trees to get material for their dams, which clog irrigation and drainage ditches, and under-

111

mine banks with excavations for dens. They also forage on corn and other crops. Beaver conservation certainly requires careful management and often prompt action to relieve damages being done.

The tassel-eared Abert gray squirrel is a beautiful animal which adds to the attractiveness of any mountain country. They are found in most of the transition zone (ponderosa pine and Douglas fir) of the state. But they were not present in the Sandia nor Sacramento mountains. We trapped and transplanted them to these mountains successfully. Now they are abundant in the Sandia Mountains east of Albuquerque.

In the late 1940's some field men and I became interested in a herd of Barbary sheep, indigenous to the moutains of north Africa, which a rancher, Joe McNight, had raised in a three-section game-proof pasture. They appeared to be fine game animals, were hardy and drouth resistant. Mr. McNight said that they had never transmitted any disease nor parasites to either cattle or sheep in the same pasture while using the same water holes and salt grounds.

We decided to experiment with a stocking on open range. Texas and California had them in enclosures, but ours would be the first open range release. We traded a dozen pronghorn antelope for a dozen Barbary sheep. My field wardens, Ray Bell, Frank Ramsey,

Marion Embrey and Paul Russell trapped the Barbary sheep and we released them in the Canadian River Gorge, a rugged canyon that cuts through seventy-five miles of north-eastern New Mexico plains country.

The planting was then supplemented with forty-seven head given to us by Mr. Randolph Hearst, Patricia Hearst's grandfather. The herd has done fairly well and made a valuable addition to New Mexico's huntable big game species—a real novelty hunting African game in New Mexico!

This concludes a summary of my wildlife restoration projects and programs while I was head of the New Mexico Department of Game and Fish.

CHAPTER TWELVE

Fisheries Programs and Projects

Fisheries is an inherent part of the operation of departments of game and fish in all states. It is more a matter of production than conservation. Of course conservation is involved in fisheries management by providing proper seasons and bag limits to keep the annual take within the available supply. Also, conservation of streams and lakes in a condition to sustain fish life by preventing pollution is an obligation in the face of its ever-present threat.

From time to time there have been instances of water pollution in this state, but we have never had the serious problems encountered elsewhere. So far as I am able to find out, there are no fishing waters in the state that are being seriously polluted today. After I retired a huge molybdenum mine and leaching plant was installed on Red River, a good mountain stream. The state's largest trout hatchery is ten miles below.

As executive secretary of the New Mexico Wildlife Federation, I got together a committee representing the U.S. Forest Service, Game Department, State Engineer, State Planning Office and others to confer with the mine superintendent, engineers and chemists about the possibilities of stream pollution. We were assured that there was no possibility of the tailings being sluiced away, getting into the stream.

Within six months after the operation began the sluice pipes paralleling the stream, which we had been told would last several years, began to break more or less regularly, emptying the powder-fine silt and noxious chemicals into the stream with resultant fish losses. Once the corporation was assessed $3,000 damages. This was an annoying situation for a long time, but in recent years the trouble has been pretty well eliminated. Constant vigilance is imperative everywhere.

It was discouraging when I entered the Department of Game and Fish to find that a number of trout hatchery sites had been

115

chosen from a political standpoint, rather than that of fish culture. For instance, the Chama hatchery site was selected by the chairman of a political party where the water supply was a spring flowing only fifty gallons of water a minute—wholly insufficient to produce more than a piddling amount of trout. Only fifteen miles away, and more accessible, was an available site with fifty times as much water of the proper temperature.

One of our first jobs was to abolish the one, acquire the other site and build a fine, big hatchery and rearing station there. That was tough with our limited funds. Fortunately, along came the federal WPA and PWA relief programs which helped us a great deal.

During my tenure we relocated three hatcheries and built one completely new one. The huge fisheries station on Red River to replace the old Taos hatchery was a gamble. There was a great abundance of spring water but the temperature was 63-64 degrees which practically all fish culturists in the U.S. and Canada thought was too warm for trout culture.

We experimented for months with trout fingerlings in live boxes in the spring water and proved that it was not too warm. Instead the rate of growth was twice what it is in the usual 50-55 degree water temperature. Experiments in hatching trout eggs were negative. The eggs hatched too fast and the fry would not live. However, fry transferred from other stations thrived and made exceedingly rapid growth in the warmer water. For a time that system was employed. Later we acquired a spring two miles away with proper hatching temperature and piped it to the site.

We gradually developed a huge plant there, and it is now one of the best producing hatcheries in the country. The growth rate is double what it is in water ten degrees colder which used to be thought ideal. My Chief of Fisheries Division, Fred Thompson, deserves much credit in the selection and development of the wonderful Red River fish cultural station.

When irrigation reservoirs were built, we always were prepared to stock them with appropriate species of fish as soon as sufficient water was impounded. While such impoundments are not ideal fishing waters, due to fluctuating water levels and small permanent pools, nevertheless they do add greatly to the fishing and boating resources of this state whose waters are quite limited.

Two outstanding examples are El Vado Lake, on the Chama River, a hundred miles northwest of Santa Fe, and Conchas Lake, on the Canadian River, a hundred and fifty miles east. El Vado is a trout water. As the lake filled we stocked it with a half million three to five-inch rainbow trout fingerlings and some fry. This stocking was repeated the next year and after that lesser numbers were

117

stocked.

As it is in most new lakes the trout growth was exceedingly rapid. In two years fishing was excellent for from ten to fourteen-inch trout. Thereafter fishing in the lake and river below, stocked by many trout going out of the lake over the spillway, became fabulous. One twenty-pound twelve-ounce trout was taken, and three to five pounders were not unusual. For a few years the lake and river below were the very best trout fishing waters in the nation.

Conchas Lake, of near ten thousand surface acres, is a warm water fish lake, and due to having a very large permanent pool, it is exceptionally well adapted to fish culture. As it filled we promptly stocked it with large mouth bass and crappie. A while later we planted pike perch. Channel catfish were in the river and natural spawning took care of that.

The U.S. Fish and Wildlife Service usually provided the warm water species upon requisition, but crappie were not available at any state or federal hatchery, so another and better way was found. I knew of a lake where crappie fishing had been excellent the previous year. So at the approach of spawning season I personally went with one of my hatchery foremen and we easily seined up five hundred nice size crappie just about ready to spawn and transferred them to suit-

118

able spawning areas of Conchas Lake.

The spawn from this planting stocked the lake and no further stocking of crappie was ever needed. It was the very cheapest and most effective fish stocking we ever did. Conchas Lake is now renowned for its bass, crappie, pike perch and channel catfish fishing.

We began the Department's fishing water development with a small dam across Taylor Creek in the Gila Primitive Area of the Gila National Forest. The site was on property owned by a sawmill operator who thought a lot of it and had the reputation of being very hard to deal with. I anticipated difficulty in acquiring the needed land at a price we could afford to pay. A mutual friend went with me to try to make a deal.

The land owner quoted an unreasonable price and took a hard-boiled attitude toward the proposed project, and I soon became discouraged. Finally, as we were preparing to leave, he said, "Barker, I'll make you one more proposition, take it or leave it."

I said, "All right, what is it?"

Keeping a poker face he said, "I'll give you all the land you need if you will name the lake for my friend here."

I couldn't believe it, but he was serious. I said, "I accept. The Taylor Creek Lake is hereby christened 'The Lloyd Wall Lake.' "
The deed was given, the dam built and we had

a new fishing lake!

The next project was construction of a dam on Cebolla Creek in the Jemez mountains to make a twenty-acre lake. We named it Fenton Lake for the homesteader from whom we bought the land. It proved to be a very good small fishing water, and being in a choice recreation area within reach of Albuquerque, it is heavily used.

Another excellent project was the surprise purchase we made of Charette Lakes at a foreclosure sale. The creditor had not expected any competition in the bidding. We caught him off guard and took him completely by surprise when I raised his twenty-two thousand dollar bid to twenty-five thousand. He was not financially prepared to raise my bid, and we got the property for a fraction of its true value.

It was a defunct irrigation project, but with no subsequent drawdowns, we made it into a real fine, fair-sized fishing water. I vividly recall the difficulty I had convincing the Game Commission by phone that they should let me have the twenty-five thousand dollars. From the time I heard of the approaching sale I had only twenty-four hours to raise the money and drive a hundred seventy-five miles to Raton. The lakes are heavily used by migrating waterfowl as well as by the public for fishing. One lake is shallow and set aside for waterfowl.

Of other projects, two small ones are worthy of mention. When I was sixteen years old I hired out as a guide to take a water engineer on a week-long pack trip into the Pecos high country, now Pecos Wilderness Area. One night we camped near a two-acre, spring-fed pond at the base of twelve-thousand-six-hundred-foot Pecos Baldy. It was the first time I had been right there. It was a marvelously beautiful area strewn with gorgeous wild flowers.

The pond was in a large basin and its outlet was through a narrow crevice in limestone formation in the bottom of the basin. I climbed down into that gently sloping crevice perhaps thirty feet to where it pinched in to a small crack through which the outlet water was gurgling. The engineer and I discussed what a nice lake could be formed by plugging up the crevice.

Twenty-nine years later when I became State Game Warden I determined to plug up that crevice in the bottom of the basin and make a big, alpine trout lake. It was several years before we could spare any money for jobs of that kind, but the first time I could spare five hundred dollars I had the job done.

We first filled the bottom of the cave-like crevice with large rocks, then tamped in rubble, then gravel on top of that. Sod was tamped in next, and then a three-foot layer of clay soil was piled over all with a team-

121

drawn slip or scraper, antecedent of the bull-dozer.

The basin filled to make a ten-acre lake about fifteen feet deep in the middle. Above that level the water broke through holes at one side so badly that we had to build a little dam to keep the water back away from that area and provide a little spillway to hold the water at that level. We had to be content with the smaller lake rather than the large one we'd planned if the basin had filled. We stocked the lake with cutthroat trout and it is now the most popular and heavily fished of the dozen lakes in the Wilderness Area.

A similar project was at Truchas Lake six miles north which I first saw on that same trip in 1902. This charming, little, two and a half-acre lake at twelve thousand feet at the base of the thirteen thousand-foot Truchas Peaks, was a bit too shallow for trout to survive in it over winter. I had it stocked several times, but the trout winterkilled. Somehow, while in the Department I never got around to building a small dam across the outlet to deepen the lake to prevent winterkill.

After I retired, I made plans and specifications for a seventy-foot long, six-foot high dam. Then, in the name of the Santa Fe Wildlife and Conservation Association, I obtained a permit from the U.S. Forest Service to build the dam across the lake's outlet. We had no money to spend on the project but determined to do the job anyway. Six men volunteered to go along with me to do the job. With modern equipment and a decent borrow pit the dam could be built in a half-day or less. But eighteen miles from road's end, a very rocky borrow pit with the work having to be done with hand tools and teams and scrapers it would take time and not be easy.

One outfitter donated the needed saddle and pack horses. Two others each donated a team of horses and a slip. Supermarkets donated the food, and a hardware merchant donated a case of dynamite, caps and fuse. The Forest Service provided the hand tools—shovels, picks, bars, etc.—and I found an old, iron beam ten-inch plow. All this had to be packed eighteen miles, but I considered myself a good, experienced packer.

For six days we worked like Trojans and completed the dam according to specifications. This required building a three-foot high, stone reinforcing wall on the outside of the dam, and riprapping the inside with suitable size rocks. Then we cut a little spillway at another place to get better circulation of the spring water.

The Game Department keeps the lake stocked with cutthroat trout and it is the nicest little lake in a majestic, scenic setting that one can imagine. There is no more winter-kill. Deepening the water by five feet took care of that.

While this is just a tiny project, its setting deep in the majestic wilderness, makes a fitting end to my fisheries development projects.

CHAPTER THIRTEEN

Acquisition of Key Areas

As funds became available, the Department of Game and Fish, in addition to prairie chicken, waterfowl and fisheries projects, began to purchase key wildlife, fish and recreation areas that would benefit wildlife and be available for public enjoyment of present and future generations. Of course, the primary value of such areas had to be wildlife and/or fish production. Even in the 1940's we could see such valuable lands being acquired for private use.

No matter what area we decided to acquire there were usually objections from livestock, timber and mining interests. But when a good tract was available and we could scrape up the money, we went ahead anyway and bought it. We were blessed with a very strong Game Commission.

Three tracts that we acquired are worthy of mention. The first is the Cimarron Canyon thirty thousand-acre area. It is a magnificent, scenic tract with Cimarron Canyon and River cutting through it for a distance of twelve miles. U.S. highway 64 follows along the meandering stream which is an excellent trout water. Wildlife on the area consists of mule deer, black bear, elk, beavers, abert and chickaree squirrels. Cougars, coyotes, bobcats and foxes are also to be found.

Excellent camp grounds along the main canyon are more or less limited. Before we acquired it, camping was not permitted except by friends of the owners. There were no public camp grounds in the entire county. This area would fill a great need, we were sure.

To acquire it we had to use all the Federal Aid to Wildlife funds available for a three-year period. The price was ten dollars an acre, or three hundred thousand dollars for the entire tract. We finally worked out a deal whereby we bought a third of the tract each year for three years. Federal regulations prevented making deferred payments.

From the outset the area became popular as a camping and picnic site, and it is now used to its utmost capacity. It is also a good fishing and limited-permit hunting unit in season. Thousand of people annually enjoy the camping privileges for a minimum camping charge.

As an investment it couldn't have been beat. Now it would probably sell for ten times what we paid for it. Other lands in the vicinity of far less attractiveness are selling for from fifty to sixty dollars an acre. But its real value is for public use and wildlife production.

It is gratifying to look back and be able to say, "We surely made no mistake when we bought Cimarron Canyon."

Another good project was on the Pecos River thirty-five miles east of Santa Fe. The American Metals Company owned considerable land there and conducted a big mining operation on it for a number of years. When they closed down the operation in 1939 I contacted the superintendent about selling the lands to the Game Department, but they were not in the notion. A couple of years later they came to me wanting to sell. I pretended not to be too anxious, but really, there was nothing I ever wanted for the Department more than that land.

There were two thousand acres, about half of it along the Pecos River and half where their mill was near the town of Pecos in the piñon hills back away from the stream. The latter tract would be of little value to us.

127

However, it did have on it a vast mill tailings dump which contained three million dollars worth of gold at the going price then of thirty-five dollars an ounce. There was no known method of retrieving the gold then.

The other tract included five miles of the Pecos River bottom land and some on side streams. They would not sell just the river property, which was what we wanted. In addition, they wanted to reserve the subsurface mineral rights on the Pecos River property and the mill tailings. The price was seventy-two thousand dollars for the two tracts subject to the mineral rights and tailings reservations. I balked at having to buy the one tract that was of little value to the Department with these reservations. Then one of the Game Commissioners, Dr. Hugh B. Woodward, joined me in trying to make a compromise. Finally, we offered to close the deal if they would give up the mill tailings reservations and they accepted those terms.

No one thought at that time that the tailings dump was worth anything because there was no known process whereby the fine gold dust could be recovered. Now, with gold worth three or four times what it was then, there is much interest in the tailings. In fact, the Game Department is currently negotiating for a share lease deal which likely could make it a half-million-dollar profit. So it may be our holding out for the compromise deal will pay off. I had a hunch it would!

As to the units on the Pecos River; camping and sanitation facilities have been installed and the area is used to its utmost capacity throughout the summer months. The five miles of excellent fishing water is open to the public where it previously was posted against fishing. Now camping and picnicking along the river bottom land is also permitted.

Like the Cimarron Canyon, the investment of seventy-two thousand dollars couldn't be beat. Some of the upland has been sold to the Forest Service for more than we paid for the whole tract. The remainder could be sold for a million dollars easily. I am mighty proud to have had a leading part in the acquisition of this land. It should never be sold. It should be kept for use by present and future generations.

The third big land purchase was the Heart Bar Ranch at the junction of the Middle and West Forks of the Gila River adjacent to the Gila Wilderness area in southwest New Mexico. The tract consists of eight hundred and thirty-six acres along the rivers which had long been used as a cattle ranch headquarters. Several hundred head of cattle were grazed yearlong under an established permit on the Gila Wilderness Area. The range was good game country— fantail and mule deer, elk, black bear and turkeys—but it had been overgrazed badly. Browse forage was in particularly bad condition.

The ranch itself was not of high value for wildlife, but the National Forest range that went with it was invaluable. The price of the land was a hundred thirty-nine thousand dollars. We had no interest in the land unless we could get a waiver of the grazing permit that would normally be issued to other qualified applicants if the purchaser of the property did not avail himself of it. Thus it was a three-way deal—the ranch owners, Game Department and the U.S. Forest Service.

Finally, we got the Forest Service to agree that if the Department purchased the property and secured a waiver of the grazing privileges the Forest Service would not issue any grazing permits for the range involved. That meant that a huge part of the Wilderness Area could be devoted to wildlife, and the range would be restored to an optimum condition. On that basis, in 1950, the Department of Game and Fish became the owner of Heart Bar Ranch giving wildlife exclusive use of a very large unit of wilderness area. It was a good deal!

Now the ranch has become accessible by a paved road from Silver City leading to the nearby Gila Cliff Dwellings National Monument. The adjacent lands are heavily used by recreationalists and the value of the ranch for such purposes has skyrocketed. I am very proud to have had a leading part in these three land and wildlife conservation projects.

CHAPTER FOURTEEN

Land Owners' Part in Wildlife Restoration and Conservation

While we hear and read a lot about private property owners' adverse attitude toward wildlife, particularly western large ranch operators, my lifelong experience while working with them in several capacities convinces me that, with a few exceptions, they have done their part, and often have taken the initiative. True, we had some difficulties with them in the early days in the matter of reducing the number of stock they were grazing on National Forests; also in obtaining adequate wildlife conservation rules

131

under the Taylor Grazing Act on the Public Domain, and in passage of the Wilderness Bill.

All that was spearheaded mainly by the organizations. When it comes to dealing with the individual rancher and farmer I have found that the very great majority are good wildlife conservationists. That is what inspired the song, "Home On The Range." The purpose of this chapter is to present the facts as to what the ranchers and farmers have done for wildlife in New Mexico and my experiences in obtaining their cooperation.

By 1900, elk had been exterminated from New Mexico and while a few of us, I as a boy and young man, wished that they could be re-established, the newly born Game Department was devoid of funds and there seemed to be no hope for it. We'd just have to wait. Then in 1910, the wealthy owner of a 360,000-acre ranch known as Vermejo Park imported from Wyoming 15 head of elk and two years later supplemented the planting with seven more. To be sure of success, the ranch owner, Mr. W. H. Bartlett, enclosed twelve hundred acres of land in an elk-proof pasture for them, and he fed them in winter as needed.

When the elk increased to the carrying capacity of the pasture they were gradually released on the open range where they thrived under the watchful eye of the proud owner. In time, they began to drift off of the ranch property in small units onto other private lands and some National Forest lands. Thus elk were first restored by a rancher friend of wildlife to both private and public land. It was shortly after that when the Game Department made four very small plantings on private lands at the request of the land owners. *It was in 1872 that Captain W. S. French made the first stocking of ringnecked pheasants on his WS ranch which is now a part of the vast Vermejo Park property.*

In 1915, the Department of Game and Fish was able to stock 37 head of elk in what is now the Pecos Wilderness Area. Two years later the Meloche TO ranch east of Raton, New Mexico, stocked 26 elk on its property. The Game Department made no further elk importations until 1938 when it stocked 24 head in the Carson National Forest and the next year added 16 more. These 40 head of elk were obtained from the Wichita Game Preserve in Oklahoma in exchange for an equal number of antelope.

In 1926, the GOS Ranch within the Gila National Forest stocked 26 elk in a five thousand-acre elk proof pasture under permit on National Forest land. The herd thrived and there was no killing of any until 1943, when the herd had reached the carrying capacity of the pasture. Then the ranch owner agreed to let the Game Department hold a hundred permit hunt, and 94 elk were taken. Through the years it was estimated that a hundred elk had escaped where trees had fallen across the fence. There were still about 200 elk in the pasture after calving the next summer.

I was State Game Warden at the time and the foreman sent for me to come down there to see if the Department would agree to having the whole 200 head turned out of the pasture onto the public National Forest range. I was tempted to throw my hat in the air and yell a big loud YES. But I contained my enthusiasm and said, "Well, if the Forest Service agrees, I guess it will be all right." The trade was made, and there the GOS Ranch entirely at its own expense had stocked public lands with 300 elk! The GOS Ranch most surely did its part in restoration of elk for the benefit of sportsmen.

In 1939, the Philmont Scout Ranch stocked 16 elk as a supplement to a small herd from a previous planting. In 1951, the Loveless Ranch stocked 26 head of elk, some of which soon drifted onto public lands. In 1966, the Block Ranch stocked 160 head. In 1955, I was employed by the owner of a 92,000-acre tract of land near Taos, New Mexico, to study the area and come up with recommendations for its use after timber cutting, then in progress, was completed. Among other things I recommended that elk be stocked there. The owner, Mr. R. M. Round, immediately sent me a check for

$1,000.00 and said, "Get all the elk you can with that." With the cooperation of the Game Department, we secured 34 head of elk and stocked them there. The area has since been acquired by the Forest Service. The Vermejo Park elk were depleted during World War II by being contributed to the meat supply in the war effort. A new owner after the war restocked the area by importing 264 head of elk.

There are other details but suffice it to say a summary shows that in the elk-restoration program, private ranchers have stocked a total of 867 head of elk and the Department of Game and Fish has stocked 683. In addition, the Jicarilla Apache Indians have stocked 318 elk on their reservation, and the Mescalero Apaches have stocked 159 on theirs.

Pronghorn antelope, originally abundant in all the plains areas of New Mexico had been reduced by 1916 to 1,700 head in some 35 scattered units and were threatened with extinction. The New Mexico Game Protective Association, organized in 1914, stepped in with a campaign to save them. There was a closed season but the law was not well respected. The GPA procured the full cooperation of the Department of Game and Fish and the great majority of ranchers in antelope areas to stop the illegal killing.

The Game Protective Association, which I joined in 1915, offered a fifty-dollar reward

135

for information resulting in the arrest and conviction of anyone killing an antelope, and paid it, too, in a number of cases. Deputy Game Warden Commissions were issued to many ranchers and sportsmen who served without pay except a $25 witness fee assessed against the law violator. I held one of those commissions from 1910 until I became State Game Warden in 1931.

Ranchers cooperated almost universally. Notable instances were the famous Bell Ranch where a sizable herd was built up. Outstanding was the Flying H Ranch southwest of Roswell. The owner, W. S. Ward, suddenly realized that there remained only 22 antelope on his 122 section ranch. He gave his cowboys and sheep herders orders to kill no more antelope and to prevent anyone else from killing antelope on his property.

Mr. Ward's orders were effective and the small herd began to increase. Later the ranch was sold and fenced coyote-proof to protect the sheep from depredations. This made it antelope-proof also, and helped the antelope as much as it did the sheep. By the mid-1930's the antelope had increased to approximately 1,200 head. This was all done by the rancher. Other ranchers cooperated just as well, but without the spectacular results. In the overall picture antelope were built up from 1,700 head to 5,000 by 1931. In the three-way efforts, the ranchers had surely done their part.

Beginning in 1937 the New Mexico Department of Game and Fish initiated its program of increasing antelope in suitable habitats where there were none. As has been stated in a previous chapter we were the first agency ever to successfully trap and transplant these swift, high-strung animals. Between 1937 and my retirement in 1953 we had thus transplanted 3,000 head, and established many new herds.

When word got out that we were about to start our antelope-trapping project, Mr. Floyd Lee, a sheep rancher near Grants, New Mexico, and President of the New Mexico Wool Growers Association came to me and said, "Barker, I want your first planting made on my ranch." That amazed me because Floyd and I had been of opposite opinions when rules for wildlife were being worked out for the Public Domain under the Taylor Grazing Act. Yet we had been friends.

I said, "Why? So you can dispose of them?"

He said, "You know better than that. They were there originally and I want to be first in bringing them back."

He got our first nine head transported in horse trailers a hundred and fifty miles, and they survived.

Another crusty sheep and cattleman was Captain B. C. Mossman who insisted on having antelope planted on his Turkey Mountain sheep ranch. The TO Ranch east of Raton insisted upon having a planting as did Ed Heringa, near Clayton, and many others. I can't recall that any rancher ever refused to have antelope stocked on his lands.

With me, most ranchers were always cooperative. Property owners have always been jealous of their constitutional rights to say who may and who may not hunt on their property. The courtesy of asking permission to hunt is definitely an obligation of sportsmen. While I was State Game Warden there was never any charge made by land owners for the privilege of hunting antelope on their property. Sometimes individual permission yes, but mostly it was whomever the Department assigned to hunt there.

Elk hunting is somewhat different and since the beginning a charge has usually been made. According to many court decisions, that is the land owners' prerogative. Back when the grazing fee for cattle was fifty to seventy-five cents per cow per month the rancher didn't feel he was out much for the elk and antelope that grazed on his lands. Now with that fee up to four dollars or more per month the situation is quite different. The property owner naturally feels that he should be reimbursed for the forage the big game animals consume.

The State is in no position to pay grazing

138

fees for all the big game ranging on private property despite the fact that wildlife is the property of the state, held in trust for the people thereof. So the property owners in most cases are charging fees, considered exorbitant by some, for the privilege of trespassing to hunt elk and antelope. When one takes into consideration the fact that, based on grazing values, fence damage, patrol and hunt supervision, it costs six or seven hundred dollars for a property owner to produce a six-year old trophy bull elk, the charges seem more reasonable.

Another example of a sheep rancher's love for wildlife is Joe McNight whose ranch lies in the rolling foot hills near Picacho, New Mexico. He fenced three square miles of pasture land with an eight-foot high game-proof fence. Then he stocked it with both native and a number of exotic species, including Barbary sheep which thrived remarkably well in the semi-desert habitat. When some of my field men and I made a study of the situation, we decided that the Barbary sheep would make a valuable addition to our big game species if stocked on open range.

So we traded him a dozen antelope for a dozen Barbary sheep to stock in the Canadian River Canyon, a very rugged, rock-rimmed gorge cutting through the plains for seventy-five miles in northeast New Mexico. There is some public land there, but most of it is privately owned. On the initial planting of 12 head there was no objection by property owners. Then the Randolph Hearst San Simeon estate in California donated 47 more Barbary sheep to supplement the twelve head. One rancher protested any further stocking, but when my friend, Ben Floersheim, heard about it he sent me word to release all of them on his big ranch which included a long strip of the gorge.

When it came to quail many ranchers co-operated by granting permission to trap birds on their property to release in areas in need of stocking. No rancher ever objected to having quail released on his property. Most ranchers do object to quail hunters entering their property to hunt without first asking permission, and some only allow invited guests.

Pheasants, of course, are an exotic species, and their habitat is confined almost entirely to the crop lands. We stocked pheasants in all the farming valleys throughout the State and never once that I know of was there any objection. But the same as for quail hunters, the farmers object to hunting without first getting permission.

There was a somewhat different situation in our prairie chicken restoration program. The chickens, indigenous only to the sand hill country of eastern New Mexico, were almost wiped out by the dust bowl conditions of the 1930's. The ground cover both of the low

140

scrub oak (Havaard Oak) and tall and short grasses was grazed down so that the necessary cover was destroyed.

To prevent that from ever happening again the Game Department set out to buy up about 30,000 acres of prairie chicken habitat in scattering tracts over the wide area. Cattlemen in the general area were opposed to the Game Department acquiring lands for that purpose. The lands were purchased anyway, fenced, water developed and some feed crops planted. Now in case of a recurring drouth the cover won't be grazed off and the chickens can survive. The acquired lands helped in restoring the birds to huntable numbers.

While I was State Game Warden I was able to get the Vermejo Park manager to permit the Department of Game and Fish to hold five limited bull elk seasons there with no charge to the sportsmen except the usual state elk hunting license.

We were also able to hold three 100 elk license seasons on the TO Ranch where the land owner made no charge. There the success percent was the best we have ever had in the State. One season a hundred hunters took 94 elk.

Some of the streams and lakes situated on private property are open to fishing by the public while others are posted. In some of the posted areas a charge may be made for fishing privileges and in other cases it is a matter of obtaining the property owner's permission.

Eagle Nest Lake with an area of over a thousand acres was impounded by a costly dam built by the CS Cattle Company. The manager of the CS Ranch, Mr. E. T. Springer, had been a long-time friend of mine, in fact we had gone to high school together. His lake was an excellent trout lake and strictly a private water, but I got him to agree to leave the fishing from the bank open to the public with him retaining all boating rights.

The lake became very popular and served the public very well for the entire 22 years of my tenure as State Game Warden, but as soon as there was a change in administration, there was no more free fishing from the shores.

These instances are not cited in an effort to picture ranchers and other land owners as little angels with wings sprouting as they drool over wildlife and the hunters who harvest it. Instead I do so to prove that most of them are at heart friends of wildlife, and that most of them have been cooperative in wildlife restoration and conservation. I've found most ranchers and farmers are reasonable, but that they are firm in their belief that it is their constitutional right to say who comes on their lands, and under what conditions anyone comes on their property to hunt or fish.

Sportsmen who are courteous to the land

owners and respect their property rights will find it highly rewarding.

CHAPTER FIFTEEN

The True Story of Smokey Bear

The Department of Game and Fish always cooperated fully with the U.S. Forest Service in Forest Fire prevention and suppression. Often we were able to be of material service. In turn, the Forest Service personnel cooperated with us in game law enforecement. Both agencies constantly endeavored to prevent litterbugging on highways and public recreational areas despite inadequacy of the laws.

Two of my District Wardens once used a clever device to effectively call attention to the need to leave a clean camp. They were patrolling one Sunday afternoon in the Jemez mountains when they came to a group of picnickers preparing to start for home, leaving a very badly littered picnic site. They stopped and cautioned the picnickers, including the Mayor of a small city, to clean up the area before they left. Later the Wardens came back by and found the area still littered with bottles, cans, cartons, plates and cups, newspapers and discarded food. It looked like they had deliberately left everything they could in resentment for being cautioned.

The Wardens filled two fair-sized cartons with the litter, brought them into Santa Fe, carefully gift wrapped them and sent them C.O.D. by express to the Mayor. Some time later I got an unsigned note which said, "Tell those damned Wardens that they made their point. It won't happen again."

Leaving camp and picnic fires without putting them out was one of the worst offences we had to contend with. One such incident caused a seventeen thousand-acre forest fire where Smokey Bear was rescued.

The spring of 1950 was very dry and windy, making the forest fire hazard greater than usual. For two days Forest Ranger Dean Earl, with a good crew of men had been fighting a fire in the Capitan Mountain in the Lincoln National Forest in south central New Mexico. Ray Bell, the Game Department's airplane pilot, had been flying reconnaissance and another District Warden was helping in charge of a squad of fire fighters.

On the afternoon of May 7, 1950 they thought they had the fire safely under control. A small crew was left to patrol the fire line and the others went back to Capitan. Suddenly the wind sprang up and a giant whirlwind swept the fire across the firebreak and quickly spread over the adjacent hillsides. Ranger Earl with his tired crew saw the new black smoke boiling up and piled into pickup trucks and rushed to the scene. Ray Bell was soon airborne to keep the ground crew informed of the fire's progress and such other information as would be beneficial to them.

By night fall, it was evident that more help was needed and soldiers from Fort Bliss, Texas, were sent. A squad of Mescalero Indians, later to become known as the famous Red Hats, were pressed into service. More supervisors were needed for the inexperienced soldiers. I sent two more of my District Game Wardens. One of these, L. W. "Speed" Simmons, headquartering at Artesia 85 miles southeast, was out on district patrol and did not get the word until he returned home that evening. Simmons was a valuable fire foreman for he had had experience fighting forest fires both in Montana and New Mexico.

He hastily got his equipment loaded, ate a quick supper and set out for the fire. He had seen the smoke boiling up and suspected

146

that he would be called. It was near midnight when Simmons arrived at the fire camp and reported to Ranger Earl for duty assignment. He was told to roll down his bed and sleep until four A.M. After a hearty breakfast, he was placed in charge of fifty Fort Bliss soldiers; a Junior Forest Officer; a cowboy on horseback as messenger and Mr. Ross Flatley, a local rancher, with his crew of four local experienced fire fighters. There was a rumor that a small cub bear had been seen the day before near the fire line, but no one had done anything about it.

Ranger Earl was worried about a hot spot section of the fire line on a steep hillside near the head of the fire lest the wind come up and carry it over the firebreak that had been made. Warden Simmons was instructed to improve the firebreak and extend it on around the head of the south side of the fire. Ranger Earl said, "Prediction is for a forty-mile wind later today and the blaze might jump the barrier, but with your experience and this crew I think you can handle it."

The crew was taken by truck before day-light to the end of the road about a mile and a half from the hot spot, then went on afoot with their tools and each with a canteen of water on his belt. Squads of soldiers were left at intervals along the fire line with instructions for improving and patrolling it. Simmons then took twenty-three soldiers and Ross Flatley's crew with him to the end of the firebreak near the head of the fire which was then burning slowly.

Suddenly at about 11:40 a terrific wind, like a jet stream, came up causing the fire, which up until then had been a ground fire, to crown out even back over a vast burned-over area. It started crowning out away back and Simmons heard the roar and saw dense clouds of black smoke sweeping their way and sensed a perilous situation. The cowboy was sent along the line to order Simmon's crew to come to him on the double, and go on back and order the mop-up squads to run for their lives out to the side of the fire. There was no possibility to use that method of escape for him and his crew.

Simmons sent Flatley to a big rock slide near the top of the ridge with orders to take refuge in it. Directly ahead was a little draw in which was a rock slide perhaps a hundred yards long up and down the draw and seventy yards wide. By the time all of Simmons's crew got to him the cloud of black smoke was engulfing them. There was no chance to outrun the crown fire in any direction. To take refuge in that little rock slide was their only chance for survival.

Simmons says, "The sky darkened with clouds of black smoke and the roar intensified. I instructed my soldiers to stay close together and follow me into the rocks, and under no

148

circumstances to try to outrun the fire. I ordered them to lie face down as close together as they could. We beat the flames by about two minutes, and I suggested that these two minutes might well be spent in silent prayer for our survival.

"We wet our handkerchiefs from canteens and held them over our faces to prevent inhalation of too much smoke. The jet stream wind swept the flames over us so hot that the treetops on the opposite side of the slide at once caught fire. The smoke became so dense that we could not see three feet. Sparks and live embers fell on us like hail. Time and again our clothes were set on fire. We had to beat the blazes out with our hands. Mine got blistered.

"It was hot as an oven and it seemed we would be roasted alive. Breathing even through our handkerchiefs was a problem. I ordered no talking and to keep heads down except to raise up now and then to see if a buddy's clothes were on fire. At the end of two long hours that we lay there we were all badly shook up. My responsibility for the inexperienced soldiers weighed heavily on me, but I had to keep calm. It was no place to panic. I'm sure we all were concerned for survival of the unit, not the individual."

Space will not permit further details of the ordeal, but after four hours the wind subsided, the smoke cleared away, embers ceased falling and the men were able to set out, partly across the burned area, for camp. The ground was still hot in spots and they had to walk gingerly. They came across cows that had burned to death. Bloated, with mouths open, hair burned off and hides charred they were not a pretty sight. One soldier exclaimed, "Except for the rock slide the Chief took us into we would look like that." The men were all pretty badly shook up, yet after supper and a fitful night's sleep, they set out again across the burned area for the fire line.

Suddenly they heard a whimpering sound like that of a sick child. What could have survived that holocaust to whimper? The whimpering continued from they knew not what or whence. Then Warden Simmons discovered a tiny, five-pound cub bear clinging to the charred bark of a pine tree. Simmons rescued him and found that his fur was singed, the soles of his feet badly burned and he was in a starving condition. They could not have foreseen that the whimpering they had heard would soon be heard across the nation and echoed down through the years!

Major Bob Cooper had come with the crew to see the sight of its previous day's ordeal. He gave the pitiful cub first aid from a kit he was carrying. Then, cuddled in a coat, Simmons sent him to camp by two of the soldiers. That cub was miraculously saved, it seems, to become SMOKEY BEAR, the most famous animal the world has ever known, and done more good than any animal that ever lived.

At camp the emaciated little cub was fed canned milk and candy which he readily ate, but they gave him far too much and he became ill. Ross Flatley came by and took the poor little fellow to his ranch for Mrs. Flatley to care for overnight.

When Ray Bell returned to camp he heard about the cub and early next morning drove to the Flatley ranch to see how he was doing. Mrs. Flatley said, "I'm glad you came, I did the best I could for him but he cried all night with a whopping bellyache."

Ray tucked the cub in a small box as comfortably as possible and took him back to camp. Everybody there had to take a peak at him and ask questions. One was, "How old is he?" Ray answered, "Bear cubs normally are born in early spring, probably he was born in March, but he is small for his age." Ray asked Ranger Earl if he could be spared long enough to fly the cub to Santa Fe for medical treatment. That was no problem for the fire, which had covered seventeen thousand acres, was now under control. Soon the cub and Ray were airborne.

From the Santa Fe airport, Ray phoned me and I met him at Dr. E. J. Smith's veterinary hospital. Dr. Smith at once took a sympathetic interest in the cub. He treated and bandaged the painfully burned feet, then gave him medicine to relieve the bellyache. Dr. Smith said, "Apart from the burns and belly-ache, the little fellow has suffered terrible shock but he still has a good chance to live." The cub was left there in the doctor's care.

At first the cub was referred to as Hot-Foot Teddy, but very soon and naturally he was dubbed Smokey after the fire preven-tion Forest Service poster initiated in 1945. The name caught on and he soon became *the* SMOKEY BEAR.

The cub's feet soon healed, as is typical of wild animal injuries, but he wouldn't eat well. One day Ray visited the hospital and his charming seven-year old daughter went along. While Ray and Dr. Smith were discussing the cub's dietary problems Ray felt Judy tugging at his coat. When Ray asked what she wanted Judy said, as if from experience, "Daddy, let's take him home, mamma will make him eat."

They took Smokey home and Judy was right. Mrs. Ruth Bell mixed pablum (an instant baby cereal) with honey and milk. Then she forced the sticky paste mixture into the cub's mouth until he decided he liked it. From then on there were no more dietary problems, little Smokey became healthy and grew fast. He and Judy became great pals, but he was cross with everyone else, including his benefactor, Ray Bell. He also made friends with the Bell's

152

cocker puppy named Jet. They romped in the yard together, ate from the same dish and shared backporch sleeping quarters.

Ray had taken Harold Walter to the fire scene for pictures before it had fully cooled off and the smoke all cleared away. His pictures were excellent and, as Smokey came into the limelight, they became a valuable historical record. Harold also took many pictures of Smokey from the beginning and they were responsible for spreading the news of Smokey's rescue. The press seized upon the situation as a news item worthy of national coverage. As a result we had many requests to sell him and donate him for worthy causes. I refused all offers and requests.

Someway it now appears that there was, from the beginning, some hazy thoughts about his final disposition. As Smokey grew, he became cross with Ray and other adults except Ruth Bell. He also became a crowd-getting attraction when exhibited at local public meetings. K. D. Flock, supervisor of the Santa Fe National Forest became interested in him. I believe I would have to say that Supervisor Flock, Ray Bell and I jointly came up with the idea of providing Smokey as a living symbol of Forest Fire prevention and wildlife conservation.

At any rate, we agreed to take that course and agreed that Flock should start the ball rolling by taking the matter up with the

Regional Forester at Albuquerque. That Flock did and we were dumfounded when the Regional Forester turned down the offer and said he could see no value in it. It would have been unethical and a violation of policy for the Supervisor to go over the Regional Forester's head and make the proposition direct to the Chief Forester Lyle Watts in Washington. However, there was nothing to keep me from doing it.

I asked Ray to get Lyle Watts on the phone with me which he promptly did. The instant Forester Watts understood the proposal that Smokey be donated to the Forest Service to become a living symbol for Fire Prevention and Wildlife Conservation Programs he became enthused with it. He called Clint Davis, his publicity director and asked us to deal with him.

I told him we were willing to donate our little Smokey who had been rescued from that terrible fire to have his life consecrated to programs for forest fire prevention and wildlife conservation and substitute for the Forest Service's fictitious symbol. Clint Davis, whom I knew personally, declared, "That is the greatest idea for beneficial publicity that I have ever heard of. Of course we will accept your offer!" From there on it was smooth sailing.

On June 9, 1950, I wrote Chief Forester Lyle Watts, outlining the circumstances of

Smokey's rescue and rehabilitation, including the episode of Warden Simmons in saving the lives of a crew of 23 soldiers. Then I said, "We are willing to release Smokey to you to be dedicated to publicity programs for forest fire prevention and wildlife conservation. .... We will be glad to let you have Smokey for these purposes. We will arrange for his shipment by airplane, but first, I would like to have an outline of the program you have for his use and care."

The State Game Commission had approved of our plan and no one had disagreed with it, unless it was the Regional Forester. We at once began to make plans to deliver Smokey to his new home in the National Zoo in Washington. We were stymied when commercial airlines refused to take him except as baggage where no one would be allowed to be with him. That wouldn't do. It would be too risky to ship such valuable and perishable property that way. Besides it would be beneath Smokey's dignity to travel as common baggage.

Obviously a private plane had to be the answer. Ray called a friend of his, Frank Hines, a Piper airplane dealer in Hobbs, New Mexico. Hines offered to help any way he could. He contacted Bill Piper Sr. and he was willing to help. They arranged for Hines to furnish the plane and Hines kindly offered to fly Smokey and his caretaker to Washington,

155

D. C.. Preparations were made for Smokey's departure at 6:00 A.M., June 27, 1950.

A local public-spirited artist decorated the plane with a fine painting of Smokey with a ranger hat and an arm in a sling on the side of the plane with the name SMOKEY in big letters along side. Since I was unable to take the time, I sent my assistant, Homer Pickens, to accompany and care for Smokey and deliver him to the Chief Forester in Washington. Smokey traveled in a small wire cage and wore a leather collar with leash attached.

News of the bear's flight preceded him, and everywhere the plane stopped for gas and overnight in St. Louis, crowds gathered to get a glimpse of the already famous Smokey Bear. Upon arrival in Washington, despite a pouring rain, a tremendous crowd was there to meet the plane and welcome Smokey to the capitol city. Included in the gathering were Clint Davis, Bill Piper, Senator Dennis Chavez, of New Mexico, other Senators and Congressmen, hundreds of Boy and Girl Scouts and many newsmen and photographers.

The next day there was a formal reception and dedication ceremonies for Smokey with many dignitaries taking part. Then Smokey was taken to the National Zoo to begin his fabulously successful career which is familiar to all. I am very proud that my men and I collectively were responsible for all of this.

156

CHAPTER SIXTEEN

Battle for the Wilderness Bill

While the concept of wilderness values dates back a century and a quarter to the days of Henry David Thoreau, it was not until the 1950's that wilderness preservation became a national issue. The controversy was provoked by introduction of a wilderness-preservation bill in Congress by Senator Hubert H. Humphrey and others, S. 1176, in 1956. Commercial interest opponents immediately became belligerent and conservationists and conservation organizations united in defence of the proposed new wilderness policy.

The idea of establishing wilderness areas within the National Forests, it seems, originated in the fertile mind of Dr. Aldo Leopold who was working in the Regional Forest Service office in Albuquerque, although others were thinking along the same line. At any rate, the first wilderness area established was the Gila Wilderness Area of nearly a half million acres in the Gila National Forest of southwest New Mexico in 1924. Dr. Leopold certainly had a lot to do with that. I attended the fiftieth anniversary celebration at the entrance to the area along with two thousand other wilderness enthusiasts on June 2, 1974.

The area was created by executive order of the Secretary of Agriculture, and not by act of Congress. The venerable American Forestry Association supported the policy, and by 1957 eighty wilderness, wild and primitive areas had been established in like manner in the National Forests, mainly in the west. The term wild area was applied to wilderness areas of less than a hundred thousand acres, and primitive areas were tentative selections pending further study or boundary adjustment, but they were administered the same as established wilderness areas.

Under that system there was a degree of instability due to the constant pressure of commercial interests to eliminate first one corner then another, and for special concessions within the areas. What a Secretary of

Agriculture can do he can undo, and there was a lurking fear that some day there might be a Secretary of Agriculture who was opposed to wilderness and that any part or all of the wilderness system might be wiped out.

Furthermore, many saw the need for establishment of units of wilderness within National Parks, National Wildlife Refuges and on the Public Domain. For these reasons public sentiment grew for enactment of federal legislation to establish wilderness preservation as a national policy, and have all wilderness areas established by act of Congress. Up until then wilderness areas had been set aside only within the National Forests.

A hearing was held on Senator Humphrey's bill, S. 1176, by the Senate Committee on Interior and Insular Affairs in Washington, D. C. on June 19 and 20, 1957. There were many supporters and some vigorous opponents. Many defects in the bill were disclosed, and it was agreed that a substitute bill should be drafted and introduced. Senate Bill S. 4028 was the result, and hearings were held on it in Bend, Oregon; San Francisco, California; Salt Lake City, Utah, and Albuquerque, New Mexico, in November, 1958.

I testified at the Albuquerque hearing for the New Mexico Wildlife and Conservation Association (now named Wildlife Federation) although there were some questionable features. Again there was vigorous opposition

159

to the bill by commercial interests, especially mining, timber and livestock. The bill did not pass.

During ensuing terms of Congress other refined and improved bills were introduced by Senator Anderson of New Mexico. I believe there were nine hearings all told by House and Senate Committees on Interior and Insular Affairs, and I testified at six of them. My friend, Howard Zahniser, Executive Secretary of the Wilderness Society, was always a key witness. Most conservation organizations presented sound testimony for wilderness preservation. The opposition continued as it had from the beginning.

Due to my enthusiasm for wilderness preservation, many individuals and some organizations called upon me to help prepare their statements. I usually presented a statement for the New Mexico Wildlife and Conservation Association in addition to testifying for myself. In addition, I presented from twenty-five to a hundred letters sent to me by friends, including many Wilderness Trail Riders.

I believe that the statement that I made at the House Committee hearing in Las Vegas, Nevada, on Senate Bill S. 4, by Senator Anderson, which eventually was passed by Congress, presents a pretty clear picture of what we were up against. After giving my qualifications to comment on the proposed legislation from a variety of standpoints—professional hunter and guide, Forest Ranger and Supervisor, rancher, game-preserve manager, State Game Warden and director of wilderness trail rides, I presented the following statement: "Mr. Chairman: This is my own personal statement. However, I am a member of a dozen or more organizations which, I am sure, fully endorse my position. Also I guarantee that my plea for wilderness preservation represents the sentiments of men and women from practically every state in the union with whom I have ridden, hiked, camped, hunted and fished in the wilderness areas.

"I have been on twenty-two wilderness trail rides sponsored by the American Forestry Association, and have been its representative in charge of sixteen of them in five different states. Those twenty-two trail rides, with twenty to thirty guest riders on each trip, brought me in prolonged contact with over five hundred average American men and women from all walks and stations in life and from all over the country.

"These people sought their recreation in wilderness areas and around wilderness campfires to get away from the stresses and tensions of modern urban life. Every one of them was enthusiastic about wilderness preservation for present and future needs. They want to see these areas kept free of commercialization of any kind so that they may be handed down to

161

our successors in the majestic condition in which God loaned them to us.

"I have been using wilderness areas ever since I was a little kid. Fifty-two years ago I took my young bride on a week-long camping trip in the Pecos Wilderness. We went again last year, and in between we have gone scores of times. We will go again come spring and take along some of our grand-children. I have ridden wilderness trails with many hundreds of others through the years on camping, picture taking, hunting and fishing trips.

"As a result, my honest appraisal is that such trips into the unspoiled, pristine, back country are not only enjoyable, but are most beneficial for recreation and relaxation of mind and body. I know of no one with whom I have ridden and camped who would disagree with that. There is nothing that provides better training for Boy and Girl Scouts, and other young folks, than wilderness trips. They are a powerful antidote for juvenile delinquency.

"It is amazing how rapidly the use of wilderness is increasing. As an example, when I was Forest Ranger on the 167,000-acre, New Mexico Pecos wilderness area in 1912 it was estimated that there were two hundred visitors to the area each year. When I became State Game Warden in 1931, the number of visitors had increased to eight hundred. The area had not yet been designated a wilderness.

Last year there were 10,000 persons who spent one day or more in the twenty-year old wilderness. Those are estimates of the State Game Department and the U.S. Forest Service. There are fifty users now where there was one fifty years ago!

"On my trip through the Briger Wilderness in Wyoming, on just one of several trails a few years ago, we encountered many other pack-in parties, a number of back-packers and a group of a hundred and one Sierra Club hikers with horse-transported camp equipment on an eight-day trip. To say that wilderness areas are too little used to be justified, as opponents of wilderness preservation do, is the utmost folly, and that the use and demand for wilderness won't increase at a rapid pace is extremely shortsighted.

"Those who claim that only the robust and hardy people are able physically to take wilderness trips, as some have done here today, simply do not know whereof they speak. The average man, woman, boy and girl can, and do, make wilderness trips. I know for I have ridden and camped with over a thousand of them from seven to seventy, and they have been just average city and country folks. They do not need to be expert or experienced riders either.

"Some opponents of wilderness preservation say that wilderness areas would be for the rich only, since they claim, only the rich

163

could afford a wilderness trip. That, of course, is pure poppycock! The people I take on American Forestry deluxe trips are, for the most part, not rich people. They are doctors, lawyers, businessmen, nurses, secretaries, stenographers, school teachers, farmers, chemists, college students, technicians and a big percent list themselves by that truly glorified title of 'housewife.' They are not rich men's wives either!

"The deluxe American Forestry Association trips only cost about twenty-two dollars a day, about what it would cost at a good hotel, without a horse. A back-pack trip can be made for less than two dollars a day, and there are several types of trips with costs in between.

"Now, as to the livestock organizations' objections. I have many good friends who summer-graze their cattle on wilderness areas and I hear no complaint from them. They are content to continue to get the best of summer grazing for half what it costs on private lands. The facts are that the livestock people are not affected by wilderness areas or the proposed legislation because every bill that has been introduced contains the specific provision that, and I quote, 'The grazing of livestock where established prior to the effective date of this act shall be permitted to continue subject to such reasonable regulations as are deemed necessary by the Secretary of Agriculture.' Of course all grazing on national forests is subject to regulation by the Secretary.

"The lumbermen, miners and gas and oil people object to wilderness preservation and also to the proposed legislation to accomplish that end in a democratic way. We should be governed by law and not be subject to arbitrary whims of a public official as it could be the way the situation now stands. The Secretary could, if he were so minded, abolish any existing wilderness area, or part thereof, within the national forests, or the whole system for that matter. That is the way the opponents want it, but the way it should be is to enact a proper law to insure preservation of an adequate system of wilderness areas for the future.

"Provision is made in S. 4, H. R. 970 and H. R. 9520 for prospecting by modern scientific methods to take care of the overall interests of the American people. Likewise there are provisions for mining, dam and road building, and in fact, for any commercial development where the President shall determine that to authorize such activity and development will better serve the interests of the American people than would its denial.

"Wilderness units within national parks and wildlife refuges are now protected by law against all such commercial encroachments. It is within the national forest wilderness system, comprising only eight percent of the

165

total national forest area, that we are primarily concerned with in that regard.

"We proponents of sound wilderness-preservation legislation have often been called selfish by miners, lumbermen and other commercial interests for wanting to save for wilderness purposes eight percent of the national forest area. Mr. Chairman, I ask who is being selfish? The ones who simply want to preserve a meager eight percent in its natural state for the benefit of present and future generations, or those who now have ninety-two percent of the national forests for regulated commercialization and exploitation and demand the other eight percent also?

"Then the charge is made that wilderness is a single use, and therefore, is inconsistent with the forest service's venerable multiple use policy. No one section of land can be devoted to all land uses. The highest use of one may be timber production, another grazing, another may be summer home or camp sites, still another may be watershed or wildlife with a certain amount of overlapping throughout.

"But wilderness is certainly not a single use. Instead wilderness areas provide many important uses. Wilderness areas are unique because they serve at one and the same time a variety of highly important purposes without diminishing or damaging the natural resources in any way. Most wilderness, wild

166

and primitive areas have a very high value for watershed purposes. Wilderness preservation provides the highest type of watershed protection. Water is the lifeblood of the west.

"Wilderness serves highly important educational and scientific purposes. It provides opportunity, found nowhere else, for some of the highest types of recreation and relaxation, sorely needed in a turbulent world—riding, climbing, camping, hiking, picture taking, meditation—in spiritually stimulating, pristine settings.

"Wilderness provides unspoiled habitat for wildlife and fish where sportsmen can enjoy their sport and recreation in uncrowded, scenic natural environments. The majestic peaks, verdant, flower-spangled meadows, alpine forests, tumbling streams and lucid lakes provide the amateur and professional photographers with unexcelled artistic subjects. Then there is regulated grazing for livestock.

"These multiple uses neither consume, damage or diminish the resources, but the areas, if preserved as wilderness, will serve posterity as well as they do us.

"I may add that posterity will surely hold us in utter contempt if we fail, before it is too late, to save enough of these magnificent, God-given outdoor natural history museums in their pristine condition for its benefit and enjoyment.

"There are those who assert that a bit of

lumbering here, some mining there, and all that goes with such operations will not impair the wilderness character of the area, nor prevent its enjoyment by wilderness riders, hikers, campers and other visitors. Those who make such claims have either never had a wilderness experience, or their souls are too dead to appreciate it. A wilderness trip with such operations going on would be like trying to enjoy grand opera with the area surrounded by jackhammers.

"In previous wilderness-bill hearings, opponents have persistently argued that we should wait for the Outdoor Recreation Review Commission, set up by Congress, to submit its report, and to act on wilderness bills before that would be premature and ill-advised. That report is now out and it sets up six categories for classifying outdoor recreation resources. Primitive areas, synonymous with wilderness, are listed as the fifth class. In several places the report recommends wilderness legislation. Wilderness was considered so important by the Outdoor Recreation Resources Review Commission that it devoted a 350-page volume to it! Are not those who said *wait* going to accept the report now? Is this Committee not going to accept its guidance?

"It seems to me that the will of the people for wilderness preservation is expressed in the ORRRC report and confirmed by the Senate's six-to-one vote in passage of S. 4. ... It is hoped that this hearing will result in getting a bill out of Committee so that the House of Representatives as a whole may vote on it.

"As to which of the several bills is best: I endorsed S. 174 of the 87th Congress and S. 4 of this session, as did hundreds of organizations and thousands of individuals throughout the country. I believe they are good bills."

Then I gave my analysis of the several bills pending before Congress, bringing out objectionable features. Then I said:

"Mr. Chairman, I appreciate very deeply the opportunity of presenting my testimony on wilderness preservation here today. In closing I would like to add a little poem of mine titled, *Outdoor Heritage*:

"The outdoors deeply lies in American hearts,
    In America's cherished traditions;
In its history, heritage, likewise its arts,
    To preserve it should head our ambitions.

When Americans search for the meaning of life,
    Or a means of escape from life's stress,
They won't find it in cities midst turmoil and strife,
    But, instead, in some lone wilderness."

After eight long years the battle for wilderness preservation was coming to an end. Public sentiment for wilderness-preservation legislation was becoming too strong for the House

169

Committee on Interior and Insular Affairs to withstand any longer. The Senate had passed S. 174 in the previous session, but it died in the House Committee. Now it had passed S. 4 and was becoming impatient with the House Committee for stalling on the popular legislation.

Suddenly the Chairman of the House Committee on Interior and Insular Affairs withdrew his objections to the legislation. Possibly it was because he needed the Senate Committee's support for a bill of his to set up a Public Lands Study Committee, or he was just bowing to public sentiment. Anyway, the wilderness legislation passed the House of Representatives in 1964, and has been functioning well ever since.

The act made wilderness preservation a national policy. All of the existing wilderness and wild areas were firmed up as such by the act. Primitive areas were to be studied and reported upon by the Forest Service within ten years with recommendation for inclusion in the system or abolition. That work has progressed well with many areas being added to the wilderness system by acts of Congress.

Also studies of other areas are being made to determine their suitability, or lack of it, for wilderness preservation. National Monuments, Parks and Federal Wildlife Refuges administrators have submitted recommendations for inclusion of many units in those areas in the wilderness system. Since passage of the legislation, use of wilderness areas has skyrocketed, presenting new problems.

In conclusion may I say that it was one of the greatest pleasures and satisfactions of my life to have the privilege of working with so many fine organizations and wonderful people throughout the wilderness preservation campaign. It was an honor to work hand in hand with Senator Clinton P. Anderson. Whatever I accomplished was due to the support and cooperation of conservation organizations and individuals, both strangers and friends. I thank God I just happened to be in the right place at the right time to lend my efforts to such a worthy cause.

CHAPTER SEVENTEEN

Future Problems in the Conservation Field

At eighty-nine I might well say that my future lies behind me to be relived in reminiscences. However, it seems possible my lifelong experiences, and lessons learned in the field of conservation may enable me to still make some contributions for the future. As long as the good Lord permits me to stay around, I am sure that I will not be content to sit back and reminisce. Unfortunately, radically changing times, attitudes and methods in these atomic, jet and Watergate days make it difficult for one of my genereation to fit in.

Veritably there are many formidable

problems to be solved and high hurdles to be cleared if Americans are to sustain the good life which is their sacred heritage. We must have pure air to breathe and pure water to drink. The soil must be conserved to provide maximum food production and forests must be managed on a sustained yield basis. Adequate wildlife habitat must someway be saved and wilderness areas preserved intact. We must have energy for industries, lights, household facilities and for travel.

It must be impressed effectively upon young folks that morality, integrity, honesty, patriotism and industry are essential ingredients of a good life. Above all, we must not forget our beneficent Creator.

I have faith that such scientists as those who produced the atomic bomb and energy, filled the air with jets, sent men to walk on the moon and provided a space laboratory for men to work and live in while orbiting the earth, can solve the energy problem. Training for and devotion of energies to work in that field, it seems to me, would serve a much higher purpose than many federally funded investigative projects such as we read about.

New Mexico is fortunate in having no serious water pollution problems. However, our long vaunted deep blue skies are now often marred by smog, and mountains over fifty miles away, formerly seen in distinct outlines, are now either hazy or invisible.

What a shame!

The Soil Conservation Service is reported to be doing a good job in many respects, and land owners and users are becoming more aware of the necessity and advantages of preserving soil resources. Yet reports indicate that this country is annually losing thousands of acres of precious farm and grazing land by erosion. So, it seems to me, the erosion-problem areas should be pinpointed and ways and means of stopping such wasteful erosion be found. We are going to need every acre of land we have before many years.

The draining of wet lands and channelizing of streams is, in most cases, detrimental to the environment generally, and destructive of fish, waterfowl and other wildlife habitat. The disastrous effects of many such projects would seem to warrant appropriate prohibitive legislation. Is there any valid need to destroy those God-made areas? Surely He had a purpose in creating them!

While National Forests embrace only a fraction of the nation's timber resources they must be managed on a sustained yield basis. It is an extremely shortsighted policy to increase the presently allowed timber harvest because of a current lumber shortage. Such a policy will inevitably result in depletion of the resource and a greater shortage later on.

We must look to the future and manage the National Forests on a sound multiple use basis. Their potential for recreational use is very great, and the demand for such use is becoming greater all the time. To devote use of National Forests to the greatest good for the greatest number in the long run on a multiple use basis will require the most careful, farsighted planning. While the public domain lands, managed by the Bureau of Land Management, differ greatly in character from National Forests, they should be managed under the same general principles.

Wildlife habitat in the west, to a great extent, is found in the National Forests and BLM lands, and it should not be too difficult to maintain it there. Yet there are some conflicts with commercial uses. The public, as well as sportsmen, should remain ever vigilant to see that wildlife gets its deserved, hereditary share.

To some extent in the west, and a far greater extent elsewhere, wildlife must depend upon friendly land owners for a place to live. Obviously it behooves wildlife agencies, sportsmen and non-hunting wildlife conservationists to work closely with land owners in encouraging them to conserve wildlife and its habitat. While wildlife is the property of the state held in trust for the people thereof, the fact that owners of the land upon which it is found have qualified rights in connection with it must not be overlooked.

Any taking of wildlife that the land owner

does or authorizes must be done in conformity with state and federal laws. However, he has the inalienable right to say who may come upon his lands to hunt and under what conditions, including such charge as he desires to make. Respect of private property and the rights of the owner is the key to wildlife production on private property and the public's privilege of sharing in its enjoyment.

The constant encroachment of highways, cities, housing developments, military reservations and many other types of development upon wildlife habitat is serious. What worries me is that it will never stop unless we see to it that habitat for wildlife is given equal weight as a public benefit in planning for the future.

A serious problem in wildlife management in the future is a growing sentiment against hunting of any species of wildlife. This idea seems to be prompted by the belief that sportsmen are out to destroy the wildlife resources. Such is not the case at all. Sportsmen want and work for more wildlife. They certainly want to preserve the resource, and must do so, or else there would be nothing for them to hunt. They and game managers are not that shortsighted.

It is, and ever has been, the sportsmen's money paid in for hunting and fishing licenses, and excise taxes on firearms and ammunition that has supported wildlife conservation and restoration programs and projects, and promoted good wildlife conservation legislation, both Federal and State. Hunting and fishing has been a vital part of the way of life ever since the days of the Neanderthal Man.

It is argued that it is wrong to kill God's creatures. I submit that fish are God's creatures just the same as deer, bear and quail are. If it is wrong to take one then it is wrong to take the other. If it were wrong to kill fish it seems inconceivable that Christ would have chosen some fishermen as his disciples, or that he would have fed the multitude with fishes!

Unfortunately, among sportsmen as among other groups there are some renegades, but that does not justify condemnation of all hunters. Memory is fresh of the prosecution of some high Government officials for their misdeeds, and forced resignation of a President and Vice President. But that is no reason to put all officials and Presidents in that class.

As examples of sportsmen being the best friends of wildlife, here are some facts: While I was State Game Warden for 22 years we had no funds except from sources above stated. Yet we increased deer from 65,000 to 200,000; antelope from 5,000 to 22,000; restored elk to many areas from which they had been exterminated in the 1800's; saved the prairie chickens from extirpation; provided and developed refuges for waterfowl and non-game birds; built lakes for fish and hatcheries to stock them, and did many other things to

177

augment the wildlife resources. The hunting and fishing fraternity paid the whole bill. The non-hunters paid nothing unless they bought a hunting or fishing license.

We all want abundant wildlife. Therefore, we must be realistic and work together to have it. Throat cutting will accomplish nothing!

Passage of the wilderness preservation act establishing a wilderness system as a national policy was a farsighted beneficent accomplishment for both present and future generations. The provision for examination of other areas within National Parks, Wildlife Refuges and the National Forests, including existing primitive areas, was equally wise. It is gratifying that the program has progressed reasonably well, and that many new wilderness areas have been, and will be added to the system established by the wilderness act.

That does not mean that we can sit back and gloat over what has been attained, for pressures to abolish or open wilderness areas to timber, mining and other commercialization will not only continue, but will become more intense. Militant vigilance will be necessary to maintain intact what we have gained through arduous labors. Wilderness is worth militant defense!

Contrary to the contention of wilderness preservation opponents , the use of wilderness areas has skyrocketed since passage of the wilderness bill. Now overuse has become a serious problem in many areas. Actually, so far it is not so much a case of overuse, but one of improper distribution of users. The tendency of wilderness users is to concentrate in the more accessible and handy areas, particularly near lakes and along the principal streams.

Actually there are many more excellent campsites in more truly wilderness settings which are seldom, if ever, used. On the New Mexico Pecos Wilderness, and elsewhere, user permit systems have been established to give Forest Officers personal contact with users and provide information and suggestions on wilderness use and distribution. To assist in the use and distribution program last year, I prepared a list of thirty-six excellent unused campsites on the Pecos Wilderness, spotted them on a map of the area and described how to get to them. That is proving helpful in getting relief for the overused popular areas.

Everywhere the littering problem is serious. On the Pecos the Forest Service operates a clean-up crew throughout the season with a pack string and packs out many tons of camp debris—bottles, cans and foil which the user should pack out himself. In our wilderness trail ride programs we establish camps away from lakes and streams as much as possible, and camp where there is an abundance of

179

forage to prevent overgrazing. We also pack out all unburnable camp debris. A good slogan is: "You packed it in full and can pack it out empty."

Enough elbow room for the future very simply means population control. Chambers of Commerce and most others seem to think that continued growth is the only way to progress. That is wrong! It is, however, the way to create more and bigger problems. Better progress can be attained by improving the quality of cities, towns, establishments and the environment than by making things bigger with more people.

I firmly believe that zero-population increase is imperative if we are to maintain high living standards and the good life. The sooner we realize that and accomplish it the better off we and future generations will be. Population controls, by whatever means attained, must be made to apply equally to all ethnic groups.

I am not competent to comment on *how* to endow the younger generation with greater morality, integrity, honesty, uprightness, patriotism, devotion to duty and abstinence from drugs. I only say that such is a necessary objective to be attained.

Today's young people are supposed to be, by and large, the smartest, with the best educational opportunities, of any generation that has ever existed. Perhaps, aided by a rearview mirror, they will work out their own destiny with flying colors. I have faith that they will meet the challenge. I have utmost faith in the future of America.

That today's generation is smarter than mine was is evidenced by the fact that, after graduating from high school they may get their Ph. D. degree in six or eight years while from the time I finished my schooling with a high school diploma, it took me 72 years to get my honorary Doctor of Law degree.

A WORD ABOUT THE AUTHOR

Elliott Speer Barker, recipient of an Honorary Doctor of Laws Degree from the New Mexico State University, was born at Moran, Texas, December 25, 1886. He came, with the family, to New Mexico in covered wagons at the age of three. He grew up on a ranch in the rugged Sangre de Cristo Mountains.

He finished schooling with a high school diploma, then was a professional guide and hunter 3 years. Next he was a U.S. Forest Ranger Supervisor ten years, worked under Dr. Aldo Leopold. Ranched for 11 years.

After that a year was spent in charge of game management and predator control on 360,000-acre Vermejo Park ranch-game preserve. His book WHEN THE DOGS BARK TREED tells the story.

From 1931 to 1953 Elliott served as New Mexico's State Game Warden. He got the Department out of politics, and greatly increased game and fish.

Barker helped organize the National Wildlife Federation, served on its first Board of Directors and 9 years as its State Representative. He was three times President of the Western Association of State Game and Fish Commissioners and one term President of International Association of Game, Fish and Conservation Commissioners.

He helped get the Wilderness Preservation Bill passed, directs Trail Rides and has had 6 books published.

www.ingramcontent.com/pod-product-compliance
Lightning Source LLC
Chambersburg PA
CBHW031431270326
41930CB00007B/658